MISSION TO KESAVARAM

How the Little Bible of
Salvation brought
good news to India

REVEREND EINAR BACH

Published by R.C. Law & Co., Inc.
579 S. State College Blvd.
Fullerton, CA 92631

Printed in the United States of America

The Great Commission Resource Library
Ft. Wayne, IN

ISBN 0-939925-56-7

PREFACE

"A Mission to Kesavaram" has not been written to entertain. It is not the polished work of a professional author. It is, however, the factual account, inspiring and encouraging, of how God overcomes human handicaps and circumstances to make the impossible become reality. How God enables His servants to do His will against incredible odds.

It is also the story of God's arithmetic. How a little book was used to multiply ten-fold the communication of the Gospel among spiritually hungry people in India. "A Mission to Kesavaram" tells how thousands have been reached for Christ because of one man's obedience to Christ, the others who followed, and the ensuing miraculous events.

To paraphrase the well known lines of "For Want of a Nail" ...

> For want of obedience a vision was lost,
> For want of a vision a servant was lost,
> For want of a servant a mission was lost,
> For want of a mission a people was lost,
> For want of a people the world was lost;
> All for want of obedience!

Einer Bach's testimony is a sermon on obedience. Dare we not take it seriously?

Great Commission Resource Library
Dr. Eugene Bunkowske, 12-31-89

CONTENTS

CHAPTER ONE

A Mission is Born

A Mission Without a Missionary

Let me tell you about a mission that has developed in Kesavaram, India.It is not possible to send missionaries to India. What a tragedy this is, for this is a land of nearly 800,000,000 people. Most of these people are enslaved by the Hindu religion; a religion which recognizes hundreds and thousands of gods, yet they do not know the True God, who is the Living God, who has created all things, and has given life, and has sustained us in life, who has loved us with an everlasting love, having provided for our salvation. But let me tell you more about this enslavement later.

A Most Unusual Mission

Let me make this comment even before I tell you about this mission. This is a most unusual mission because it is developing in a land where we cannot send missionaries. This story is not intended, in any way, to discredit the many and various mission programs that have been initiated by various

1

churches where they first sent missionaries into the field, hoping they would be able to establish the church. Most of us who are Christians today would not have become Christians if the church had not sent out missionaries in the first place. The unusual thing about this mission is that it is developing without sending a missionary into the country. I might explain that ever since the people of India got their freedom from Great Britain the government of India has not allowed churches to send in missionaries. It seems that the people of India regarded the church as being British, and what was British had to go. They did, however, allow the church activities that were present in India to continue with the staff that was there. But it has been extremely difficult, if not impossible, to send in replacements. I was able to visit India as a guest on a 90-day visa in 1979.

Some people have been able to enter India as medical missionaries with special emphasis on medical work, and some have been able to secure visas as teachers. In this way some Christian ministry has continued to develop in India. It is possible, however, for someone to leave India for theological education and return to India, and for such a person to establish a Christian ministry without any interference from the government. However, most of the people that come to America to improve their education do not return to India. Most of them prefer to stay in this country rather than return to the poverty of India. So it is that many who come to this country to study theology do not return if they can find ministry in this country. The same is true of many other professional people. Why should they return to India when they can earn up to 100 times more in this country?

How "The Little Bible of Salvation" Came to Be!

Now let me continue with the story. Let me go back to the very beginning, for everything must have a beginning. It all began back in 1970, when I was a patient in the hospital at Lincoln, Nebraska. I had encountered severe kidney stone attacks. For seven days and seven nights I lay in the hospital with excruciating pain, without any relief. Morphine every two hours could not subdue the pain. I said, "Lord, let me die, or show me that there is something to live for." The next day a young man who had been in the hospital for a twenty-four hour stay stood by my bed and said, "I see that you are a minister. I've never gone to church or Sunday School or anything like that. What is it all about?" I told him if he would listen for five minutes I would tell him. I spoke to him directly about salvation the best I could. The next day I told my wife, Arda, what had happened. I said, "What we need is a little booklet that speaks plainly and directly about salvation, to give to such people, because in all likelihood we will never see them again. When I get out of here I am going to publish such a booklet to help establish a clear witness about the Christian faith." I wrote the first manuscript and sent it to Dr. Ted Raedeke, who said, "This booklet should be published."

This eventually led to the publication of the "Little Bible of Salvation," which has been used by many people in our country to help them with their personal evangelism. It is still being used by many people. Little did I realize that it would find its way to India and there become responsible for establishing the mission which I am about to describe.

How the Booklet Found Its Way to India

I left some copies of the booklet with the Concordia Tract Society in St. Louis, Missouri. A young man from India wrote to Concordia Tract Society and asked for free literature to

4

give to the people in India as he tried to establish a Christian witness among the people. "The Little Bible of Salvation" was thus sent to India.

When this young man, whom I now introduce as Peri Sastry Mandapalli, received "The Little Bible of Salvation," he said to himself, "This booklet could do us some good if it was translated into the language of our people." He wrote to me and asked permission to translate the booklet into the Telegu language. I gladly gave him permission. Of course, he wanted some money to help him with the publication. I wrote to him that I must first see the manuscript. He sent it to me. I could not read a word of it. I sent it back to him and told him to proceed with the publication. I could not send any money until I saw the printed booklet. He sent the booklet printed in the Telegu language and we were in business. The booklet is being published by the Lutheran Braille Workers in California, and is being made available in large print for free distribution among the people in India. The booklet has also been translated in Hindi, Tamil, Malayalam, Urdu, Lambadi, Koya and Oryia. To date the Lutheran Braille Workers have made 200,000 copies of the booklet available for distribution in India, but it is in Andhra Pradesh, where the Telegu language is used, that our mission has developed.

The Mission Began at Kesavaram

After we had been in communication with Peri Sastry for some time, he told me about an orphan project that he was maintaining in Kesavaram. I began to send him some used clothing which our church people graciously provided. I also sent him $30.00 a month to help take care of the children at the orphanage. I did not share this information with anyone in particular, because I did not know for sure if he really had an orphanage. We continued to support the mission as well as we could, providing especially the "Little Bible of Salvation" for free distribution. Various evangelists came to Peri to secure the little booklet to give to the people, and so the mission at Kesavaram had its beginning.

CHAPTER TWO

Is It Real?

A Visit to India

In October 1979 I was privileged to make a trip to India, courtesy of India Bible League. This is an organization worthy of your support and prayers. Their intent is to make the Bible available to every home in India, which is no small task considering the multitude of people living in India and the many languages and even greater number of dialects used by the people. English is the official language of the nation, but the people in the various states prefer to speak in their own language. Very few of the people can speak in more than one of the native languages. Only twenty percent of the adult people have any education. None of these can carry on a conversation in English. English is used only by the educated people and even these prefer to speak in their own native languages. So it is extremely difficult to make the Bible available to all the people.

I was privileged to make the trip to India as a guest of the India Bible League. They had heard about my interest in India and the "Little Bible of Salvation" being used in India.

I was very grateful to be a guest of the India Bible League and to make the tour with them. There were twenty-four men in our tour group, most of them were pastors of various

6

denominations. All of them were concerned about making the Bible available to the people in India. It was very important that we should go on the tour, that we might have some insight concerning the life and culture of the people of India, and have some understanding about the religious practices of the people, and the history of the people. I will share some of this with you before I give you a report on the mission in Kesavaram.

What a Way to Go!

We traveled by Air India from New York in a 747. I had never been in such a huge plane before. Once we were in the air it was like we were motionless in space. I sat down to relax because I knew that it would be a long flight. Service in the plane was beyond my expectation. They fed us more than we could possibly eat. It was as though we should stock up on

food against less satisfying meals later. I must say that we were truly well provided for while we were guests of India Bible League throughout our stay in India. We received instructions immediately that we should not eat any fresh fruits or vegetables, because we would likely get "Delhi Belly," which is the same as "Montezuma's Revenge," but much worse. Once you get it, it is very diffi-

cult to get rid of. I wanted to tell you about the attention we received while we were on the plane. There were these beautiful angels walking up and down the aisle of the plane, asking what they might do for us. All this time I had come to believe that angels had blonde hair. Already I had come to realize that the young ladies of India are quite beautiful, but I hadn't seen anything yet, for the most beautiful girl in all India, so far as I am concerned, was to be found at our mission. I will show her to you now and tell you more about her later.

On the Streets of Delhi

We stayed at a hotel in New Delhi for a couple of days and became acquainted with the noise and the smells which we soon learned were a part of India. We went downtown on Saturday afternoon in Old Delhi, and began to mingle with the people. We were told to keep one hand on our billfold at all times, because in the crowded streets of Delhi it would be very easy for someone to lift the billfold from any pocket. As we were walking down the street, John DeVries, our tour guide and director, was walking ahead of me about three or four feet. Three gypsy women approached me and asked me for some money so they could feed their little ones. One would bump me on one side, and get my attention, and rub the stomach of the baby and then plead with such longing eyes saying, "Bashee, bashee." I don't know what she was saying, but there was no question that she wanted me to give her some money. We had been told never to give anything to the beggars, for this is a very lucrative business in India, which I will tell you about later. By the time I had convinced the first woman that I was not going to give her anything, the second one bumped me on the left side and began the same ritual. Finally, when they were convinced that I would not help them, they ran ahead of me and made contact with John

DeVries. It was then that I saw that there were three of them and that the third woman did not carry a child. She had her hands free for action. One of the women bumped John on the right side, and the other bumped him on the left side, while the third one made a pass at his wallet. They had noticed that he was carrying his wallet in the back pocket of his trousers. They didn't even bother to do much begging. When I saw the third woman make a pass for his wallet, I jumped ahead in the crowd and touched him on the shoulder and said, "They almost got your wallet."

It wasn't all that bad all of the time. One of our men had left his camera equipment on the plane as we were being escorted into the airport. He did not notice that he had left his camera until we were at our hotel. He took a cab back to the airport and told the officials what had happened. Sure enough, it had been turned in, and he was able to make identification and receive his camera. I had a similar experience which I will tell you about later. But we must now get back with our tour group for we had many things to see while we were on this tour.

You Must See the Taj

The next day we were scheduled to see the Tajmahal. Everyone who visits India must see the Taj. What a magnificent building this is! It is truly one of the seven wonders of the world. It was built by the mogul emperor about 450 years ago to honor his wife, whom he loved very much. She had died at an early age, having given birth to some 18 children. This was really her tomb and it was built by the emperor to show his love for his wife. It was made of white marble brought down from the mountains. It took 20,000 men some twenty years to build the Taj. While it is really a tomb for the emperor's wife, it is also somewhat of a shrine, for there are those present who suggest that you might give a gift, or purchase some flowers and present them as an offering. The suggestion is made that such gifts will surely please the gods and your soul will be graciously rewarded the next time around. While it is certainly a magnificent building and the people regard it as a monument to "love," and that is certainly a noteworthy thing, if it might be used to promote love. I found it somewhat difficult to appreciate the more noble qualities of the building, realizing that it was essentially built by slave labor. Oh, the people were not really slaves, they probably received a rupee a day for their work. That is about 10 cents in American exchange. To me it seemed to be economic slavery. But on the other hand, the people had a job for some twenty years, and they were able to buy rice, so it was not all bad. I just could not get over the fact that, even today, most of the people in India work for ten or twelve cents a day.

On to Madras

But let us now fly to Madras for a visit. There we visited the publishing house where the Bibles were being printed for India Bible League. It was fascinating to see this publishing house and see the number of people doing manual labor at this plant. Here we saw the Bibles being produced. It bothered us somewhat to learn that an equal amount of literature was being published for the communists. The rest of the publications were for such magazines as *Time* magazine and the like. The one thing I noticed was the unique craftsmanship of the artists that were working for the publishing house and the magnificent color which was used in the Indian publications. Finally we came to the conclusion that color must have originated in India.

Project Philip

In Madras, we also visited a mission in the heart of the city where people had come to receive their first copies of the Bible from the India Bible League. They first had to prepare a study course and show their interest in learning what the Bible teaches, before they were given their first Bibles. The Bibles are not made available to the people unless they show much interest, for there is no way that the India Bible League and all the Bible societies in the world could supply the Bibles for all of the people that would ask for one. We met in a small room in downtown Madras late in the evening. How we were able to get through the mob of people on the streets in our bus without running over the people remains a mystery to me. Horns were blaring constantly. It was said that buses travel more by horn power than by gas power. The small room in which we met was crowded from wall to wall. Standing room only! Finally the police had to come to keep people from entering the room and trampling us to death. Surely there must have been 300 people in the small room and another thousand people standing outside looking through the bars of the windows to see what was going on. The people are very curious and will come to any gathering by the hundreds. But these people had come to witness some thirty-five people receive their first copy of the New Testament. This is a land that has traditionally rejected the Gospel, but everywhere we went people would ask us about Christianity. We began to realize that something is happening in India. I will say more about that later.

Sunday Morning Worship

On Sunday morning we went to church at a college chapel where students were preparing to become Bible teachers. They were taking a two-year Bible course. Part of their training consisted in going out on the streets, at least twice a week, to witness to the people and persuade people to enroll in a Bible study course known as "Project Philip," which is sponsored by the India Bible League. It was an interesting worship service. It was in English. Bill Scott, who is in charge of India Bible League in India, was the speaker. The men sat on one side of the church, and the ladies sat on the other side. I envisioned that I had gone back in time some forty years and was worshiping in a Lutheran church in America where this was a custom at that time. I thought to myself that these people might even become "Lutheran" some day.

Mingling with the People

After the service our men visited with the young men outside the chapel, but the women went immediately to their dormitory. It is not regarded as proper in India for women to speak with men in public. But I noticed that the women did not go into their dormitory. They stood outside in a group watching what was going on. They didn't want to miss anything. So I went over and spoke to them. I asked if any of them could speak Hindi. I gave them a few copies of the Hindi translation of "The Little Bible of Salvation." Then I asked if anyone could read Telegu, and being assured that they could read Telegu I shared a few copies of the Telegu translation. It was not possible for me to give a copy to each of them so I suggested that one might read to the others. While all of them could read, much learning takes place in India by one person reading and the others listening. There simply is not very much literature available for the people in India, so most learning is done by listening, which is not all bad. Our people in U.S.A. have almost lost the art of learning by listening. In India eight of ten adult people cannot read. The only way that they can learn anything is to listen. Whenever someone receives a copy of "The Little Bible of Salvation," at least ten people stand around and say, "What does it say?" For every 10,000 copies of the booklet that is made available 100,000 people become acquainted with the message of salvation. It is safe to say that for the 200,000 booklets that have been made available in India, 2,000,000 people have heard about the Lord Jesus and His salvation. Once again, I want to thank the Lutheran Braille Workers for what they have done in making the booklet available in large print in the various languages in which is has been translated.

Literacy

Although eighty percent of the adult population of India cannot read, eighty percent of the children are receiving a good education, and will be able to read. The children complete their high school education when they are sixteen years of age. Those who can afford to go on to higher education are very proud of their education. In fact, all of the people are very anxious to learn. There will be some great changes taking place in India during the next two decades. The young people will learn that the rest of the people in the world have a higher standard of living than the people of India. They will want to improve their lifestyle. This will be difficult because the Hindu culture teaches them that they should be satisfied with life as it is. In fact, they offend the gods if they try to improve their lifestyle and try to enter a higher caste. Nonetheless, the young people of India are asking, "What about Christianity? What does it have to offer?" They are beginning to embrace Christianity as a new way of life. But there is also another ideology that is striving to gain control of the people. They will say to the young and the restless, "Overthrow the system. Rise up against the government, and we will liberate you, and give you freedom, and increase your standard of living." As I see it, India will either become Christian or communist within the present generation. One thing that is favorable for Christianity is that the people of India are religious people. As Hindus who worship more than 300,000 gods, they have more than

300,000 reasons not to espouse communism.

St. Thomas Church

But now we join the group once more. We visit the St. Thomas Church in downtown Madras. It is said that this church can trace its origin to St. Thomas, the Apostle. I do not doubt it at all. It was a very interesting group, and although we did not have much opportunity to learn about their doctrine, we did observe that there were many similarities to the Roman Catholic church, or even the Lutheran church, perhaps it is more similar to the Greek Orthodox church. But as I say, we did not have the opportunity to get acquainted with their doctrine. It was obvious that this was a solid Christian group. There seems to be no evidence that they have ever had any connections with Western churches. It was also obvious that this church had not gained any substantial foothold among the people of India. Somehow it had not been able to penetrate the Hindu culture and traditions. This group was very eager to work with India Bible League and help to make the Bible available to the people.

Other Christian Churches in India

We also visited several of the large churches in India. Here we came to realize that the churches, built by the British during the time that India was under British control, had remained quite British; for they had been built by the British, for the British. Very few of the Indian people had ever joined these churches. So when the people of India gained their freedom they would have nothing to do with these churches. They regarded the church as being British. Very few of the Indian people had become Christian, so the churches were virtually empty. The government of India has not allowed churches to send missionaries to India since they gained their freedom. They did, however, allow such church groups and church organizations as had been established in India to continue their activities, but the churches were not allowed to send in replacements for the personnel when they reached the age of retirement. This action has been regarded by many as open opposition to the Christian churches. While there no doubt has been some opposition, and even at times some grievous persecution which has taken place in some areas, for the most part the people in India are quite tolerant of other religions. The people who have become Christian in India are permitted to carry on their ministry as long as they do not attempt to thwart the government. Perhaps it is a blessing in disguise that the church must resort to native ministry. The native people are much more capable of ministering and witnessing to their own people. The thing which we did observe is that everywhere we went the people would ask us about Christianity. they would say, "What does Christianity have to offer?" This seems rather strange, in that India has not been receptive to the Gospel during all these centuries. It is quite well established that the Christian population of India is less than four percent. It varies from state to state. In some places as many as twenty-eight percent of the people are Christian, and in other places it is as low as one-tenth of one percent. But that the people were asking about Christianity is an indication that something is happening in India. By the way, India Bible League and all the Bible Leagues put together, are not able to meet the demand for the Scriptures in India. Something is definitely happening in India. I will say more about this later.

A Warning About Kesavaram

While we were in Madras we met with many of the people who were involved with the distribution of the Bibles in India. We met a young man who was from Kesavaram, and when he learned that I was planning to go to Kesavaram he said,

"Don't go into Kesavaram alone. You won't come out alive."
He was a native of Kesavaram. This did not present a very
pretty picture for me. The rest of the pastors on the tour said,
"Forget about Kesavaram and come back to the States with
us." Of course, I was tempted to go back with them,
especially after our last evening together and the pastors
began to sing about "Old Folks at Home," and "Carry Me
Back to Old Virginy." I wanted very much to go home with
them. I told them that I was going to go to Kesavaram if it
would be the last thing I ever did. I wrote to Arda about this
and told her that I was determined to go to Kesavaram at any
cost. I think she wrote my obituary at that time in her diary. I
don't really know because I have never read her diary.

We still had to fly from Madras to Bombay by way of
Bangalore. Our stop at Bangalore was for rest and relaxation.
Bangalore is a very beautiful city, the home of the Indian Air
Force. The temperature here was quite tolerable. It had ranged
from 80 degrees at night to 120 degrees during the day almost
everywhere we went, but here at Bangalore it was at least 10
degrees cooler.

Hazards of Travel

When we were ready to board the plane at Bangalore, the
customs officials were not going to let us board the plane,
because most of us were carrying two parcels. We had been
carrying them on and off the planes everywhere we went in
India. But now one of the officials saw an opportunity to get
some extra money from each of us. Gene Goulooze, the one
who had made all of our flight arrangements, told us to stand
in line and let no one board the plane until we got clearance.
He went to the officials and talked with them for some time.
In the meantime, the plane waited for us to get clearance,
because we were scheduled to fly on the plane. If they did not
take us along they would lose money. When Gene returned he

had secured clearance for us. We asked him how he worked that out. He said he reminded them that we were guests of India and this was no way to treat their guests, and he would most surely take this up with the American consulate. When he came back he told us to step aside and let the other passengers board the plane before we got on. We were very thankful that we had someone with us us who knew how to handle such matters.

On to Kesavaram

The next day I left for Hyderabad and then on to Visakhapnam. Before I left, I asked all of the pastors to pray for me every day until I should return to the States. The I would write to them and tell them how I fared in Kesavaram.

I arrived In Visak (Visakhapatnam) the following evening, and was met by our director, Peri Sastry Mandapalli, and one of the evangelists. We stayed in Visak that night and boarded the train for Kesavaram the next day. There were thousands of people at the train station. I think the passenger train was at least a mile long. I had never seen such a long passenger train, and it was crowded to the hilt with standing room only. It was a matter of a four-hour trip to Rajahmundry. It was late afternoon before we arrived in Kesavaram. In fact, it was dark by the time that we arrived at the Bible Centre. One small room of the Mandapalli house had been made available as a Bible Centre where the booklets were kept and whatever else was available for reading. I was welcomed by the family, of course. I had to have some tea and cookies. Then I should go on to the hotel, where I was to stay for the night. As soon as I got outside of the house a mob of people came with sticks and staves and torches, and were threatening all kind of harm. I was told that our director was a "good-for-nothing," a scoundrel, and that I was wasting my money by helping him. I could see that they had no intention of wishing me well.

Already I had observed that they had broken the headlights on the taxi. Midst all the shouting and raving, I told them, in no uncertain terms, that if they did any damage to the Bible Centre, I would have Peri report them to the officials and they would be thrown in jail. And I did not care if they ever got out. I told them I knew who they were and I knew why they had come. They had heard that Peri had received some money from one of our churches in Oklahoma. His house-boy had told them about this. I had already received a letter from them by way of the church in Oklahoma, in which they were degrading our director. I told them that I had not come to argue with them, and if they would be so kind as to be on their way, I likewise would be on my way. When they first came at us with their sticks and torches I was reminded of what I had been told, down in Madras, that I would not get out alive. I did not know whether they would pay any heed to me when I threatened to have them thrown into prison. But if the Lord sent His angels to help Gideon in his battle against the enemy, I reckoned He could spare a few angels to take care of me, if not for myself, then surely for the sake of the mission which I was convinced He intended to establish. I assure you I didn't sleep that night, for I had no assurance they they would not return during the night.

The Orphanage at Kesavaram
    The next day, however, I was with the Mandapalli family. I was to visit the orphanage before we began our convention. Now I was among friends who treated me as though I were some kind of god. I had come to Kesavaram, in part, to see if the mission was a viable mission, and if indeed there really was an orphanage, or whether this was just one of many scams that exist, by which people extract money from well-meaning people, to support a project that does not exist. When I came to the orphanage it was in the evening. The

children had just been fed their daily bowl of rice. Peri quickly told me that there were many more children there that were not children of the orphanage. He had allowed some children from the street to come and have a bowl of rice also. The orphan children, however, gathered round and sang some Christian songs and brought their "leis" to place around my neck. I knew for sure these were Christian children by the songs they sang, although I did not understand any of the words. I saw small boxes lining the walls, about 18 inches long, 8 inches deep, and 12 inches wide. Each box had the name of a child on the lid. This was their hope chest, which contained all their possessions. I knew these children lived there and that the orphanage was real, but it was difficult for me to understand that 30 of these children slept in two small rooms on the dirt floor, without any covers or anything to sleep on. I was resolved that when I got home I would do something about this. So I asked the ladies at my church at Wessington Springs, South Dakota, to prepare small blankets to send to these children. We set up a support program of ten dollars a month for the support of each of the children. I will say more about this later.

CHAPTER THREE

The First
Convention of
"The Little
Bible of
Salvation"

Let's Change the Name

The next day we drove to the town where I would stay for the next six days. From there we would drive by taxi to a village of Kaldari where we were to hold the first convention of "The Little Bible of Salvation." They had advertised this as "The Rev. J. Einar Bach Memorial Bible Centre Convention." During the convention I persuaded them to drop my name from the official title and simply call it the "Salvation Bible Centre Convention." This they were reluctant to do, because they wanted so much to honor me as the "founder" of the mission. But I said that the people of India did not know me, and my name meant nothing to them. We should rather honor the Lord Jesus and call it "The Little Bible of Salvation Center." They finally agreed to this.

The convention began with twenty-four evangelists and eight Bible women and their families being present. Several other evangelists stopped in for a day or so, so that in all there were at least 40 evangelists at the convention. Most of the evangelists stayed for the six days. What a welcome was extended to me! A convention centre had been built for the occasion. It was built of bamboo poles and a thatched roof covered with palm leaves. It was strictly air conditioned, which means that the air was as hot inside the building as it was outside. "Welcome speeches" were made by several people. And, of course, I was to speak to the people. What a wonderful experience it is to speak to a group of people when you do not know their language, and very few of them know any English! Everything that I said had to be interpreted for them as I spoke.

A Language Barrier, But No Joke

I began by telling them that I had some fear as I was coming into their midst. They knew about the assault that had taken place at the Bible Centre. I thought I would pass it off with some humor. Peri Sastry had written many letters to me in the preceding years. He always addressed me as "the most delicious saint of the most High God." So I thought this would be an occasion to break down the tension with a bit of humor. I said, "In our country something delicious means that it is good to eat. Since I had thus been threatened I wondered if you were going to eat me alive." They didn't think it was a bit funny. I went on to explain to them that we should rather say, "most precious saint," than "most delicious saint." So ever since then I have been known as the "most precious saint of the most High God." I mention this not just because of the incident that took place, but to show you that our English is not always the same as theirs. However, we did not have too much trouble with language. They did say that my English was easier to understand than the British English. Sometimes when Peri was translating for me and was searching for just the right word, someone from the audience suggested what I was saying, so I observed that many of the evangelists could also understand some English. But there were some that could not speak a word of English.

Basic Christian Faith

During the six days of the convention we talked about very fundamental things of the Christian faith, such as God, the Bible, the Lord Jesus and salvation, baptism and the Lord's Supper, and life hereafter. We kept the conversation on a very elementary level. I remember a question that was asked on the day that we talked about baptism. One of the men asked, "What about re-baptism?" Now I didn't have access to a theological library, but I had my Bible and the passage come to mind where the Apostle speaks of "One Lord, one faith, one baptism." When I explained to him that baptism is "for the remission of sins," and this forgiveness is for a lifetime, I said, "There is no need for re-baptism, otherwise one might conclude that we should be baptized every time that we sin, and there would be no end of baptism. Therefore, the Lord said, 'One baptism'." I told him it was not proper that anyone should go about questioning anyone's baptism. He thanked me very much, and apologized very much that he had brought it up. I assured him that this was the very reason why we were having such discussions.

The next day I talked with them about the Lord's Supper. I did not know where these people were in such matters, because I saw little or no evidence of an organized church.

But non-the-less, I would talk with them because I did not know if I would ever see them again. So I asked them if they had the Lord's Supper. "Oh yes, when we come together at conference." Plainly, it was for Christians only, and for such as knew what it was about. So I asked them what words they used when they had the Lord's Supper. I was aware that these people had very little contact with traditional Christianity, and probably had never heard about the theological controversy that has existed in the Christian church down through the ages concerning the Lord's Supper. Most of them had never heard of Luther and I doubt that any of them had heard of Zwingli or Calvin. But what a beautiful answer I received from them when I asked them what words they used when they had the Lord's Supper. "Why, the words of the Bible, of course." What a beautiful faith these people have! If the rest of the Christian world would simply accept the words of the Lord Jesus, what a great unity there would be among us.

Rest and Relaxation

We usually had some time in the afternoon for rest and relaxation. A small room had been provided for me where I could rest. There was a small cot and a chair for me and an electric fan to move the air. Most of the time the fan did not work because the electricity would fail. This happens all over India at least twice a day. Many of the large industrial corporations have their own private electrical plants which they use when the power fails. A young girl came to my room to fan me. Her name was Sujaya Mandapalli, brother John's oldest daughter. I suppose that she was about nine years old. She stood by my chair and waved the fan in front of me, and after a while she would put the fan in her other hand and continue fanning I said, "Don't you ever get tired?" She didn't seem to understand me, not that she did not understand English, but she didn't seem to know what it was to be tired.

Children in India do what they are told to do and stay with it. Her parents had told her to do this. Besides, she was the only one that was privileged to be in my room. She was not about to give that up for anything.

A Prayer Request

One afternoon a lady came to my room. She wanted me to pray for her. She was pregnant and had a fever and headache, and who knows what else. So I prayed for her and her little one, and then I gave her some of my protein tablets that I had with me, and I told her to take one every day. I knew that they couldn't do her any harm and besides if she got well I would be like "God" to her. When she had gone from my room, Peri asked me how I knew what she had wanted. He knew that she could not speak any English, and that I could not speak Telegu. I said it was not difficult to know what she wanted. She had rubbed her forehead and patted her stomach and folded her hands and looked up to heaven. There was no question what she wanted. She wanted me to pray for her and her baby.

Shopping

We also found time to do some shopping. One afternoon we drove into a nearby town to shop. The Mandapalli girls were going to shop for a sari for Arda. I told them that I had already purchased a sari for her. I had been told by the pastors when I had made my purchase some days earlier that I would be sorry. Well, I watched the girls shop. Peri told me that they were good at such things. The merchant laid all kinds of fine silk out on the floor before us. We all sat on the floor. Bargaining continued until I thought the girls would never make up their minds. But they had already made up their minds. They waited until the price was right. When they had made their purchase and I found out how much they had paid,

I found out that I had paid exactly twice as much for the sari which I had purchased a few days earlier. Was that what the pastors meant when they said, "You'll be sorry"?

A Sunday to Remember

The next day being Sunday I preached at our convention centre, and then I was asked to preach at a couple of the mission places that afternoon. But first we were invited out for dinner. We were guests in the home of two spinster ladies, who were teachers in a public school. Now that they had become Christians they wanted to be a part of our mission group. What a spread they laid before us. We sat at a table with the finest silverware that I have ever seen. The ladies spoke of their poverty, but theirs was the only home that we saw in India that had inside plumbing and hot water in a faucet. They had prepared special food for me because they knew that I did not like curry. So I was served sweet rice. I ate my food with the silverware, but Peri poured curry sauce on his rice and mixed it with his hands and ate with his fingers. After the meal many thanks were spoken. The ladies wanted to give me another sari. I said, "No." I did not want them to do this because I already had two saris. When they learned that our daughter Eunice had been taking care of an orphan boy in India, the lady said, "Give the sari to my sister Eunice, because she loves the poor people in India." These ladies were supporting an orphan and providing advanced education for the girl who now was studying to become a doctor. Oh yes, there are some lovely people in India. When I had returned home, one of the ladies wrote to me and said, "When you were in our home we felt like the Lord Jesus Himself was a guest at our house."

One Was a Leper

Oh yes, we were on our way to preach at a couple of

mission places. At the first place we met outside of a home in the shade of the house. It was too hot to meet in the house and it was also too dark. I suppose there were 36 or 40 people there. I spoke to them about the Lord our God being the true and living God. I told them that the gods of the Hindu people are idols, and that they are idle. They have never been alive, and therefore, these gods could do nothing for them. I told them it was altogether foolish for them to worship such gods that can do nothing, but that our God is the "living God" who has created us and given us life. He sustains us with life, and loves us, and has provided for our salvation by sending us the Lord Jesus to become our Savior. The preaching was very elementary. It was interpreted for the people by brother John, Peri's brother. After the sermon, I was told that some of the people were requesting baptism. It was not as though I had preached such a powerful sermon, although I must admit when it is translated, it becomes quite a message. These people had been prepared for baptism by the evangelist who had taught the people from "The Little Bible of Salvation" about the Lord Jesus. And they wished to honor me by asking me to baptize them. There were three women that came forward for baptism. After I had baptized them, there was a man that came from outside the assembly, who requested baptism. I learned later, after I got home, that he did not sit with the rest of the people because he was a leper. So I also baptized a leper.

Twenty-eight Baptisms at One Service

That same afternoon, we went to another part of the city and held a service on a hilltop where the people met in a building, or should I say under the roof of a building. It was one of those air-conditioned buildings which had no walls. There were about eighty people in this group. I preached a similar sermon. Again, after the sermon I was told that some people were requesting baptism. This time each one wanted me to give them a name from the Bible, so they would no longer be known by their Hindu name. Each one agreed to a name before they received baptism. The people kept coming and coming. Soon I was fresh out of names. I had not been prepared for something like this. I baptized twenty-eight people at this service. Again, all of them had been prepared for baptism by the evangelist, who had used "The Little Bible of Salvation" in his teaching. It was a very impressive service which I shall never forget.

And They Kissed My Boots

After the service we took some pictures and I said goodbye to the people. I started down the cowpath to the taxi. Soon I heard the rushing of the people behind me. I grabbed, instinctively, for my billfold, for we had been told to keep one hand on the billfold all the time we were in India. These people did not want my billfold, they just wanted to touch me. Then I said goodbye to them again, and turned to go down the path once more, but I could not move because three or four men had fallen down at my feet and had grabbed me by my legs. They were kissing my boots. It was not just because my boots had come from Texas and deserved some recognition, but they were so glad that I had come to visit them and preach for them. By the way, I kept my money in a special billfold in my boots all the time that I was in India. But these people did not know that. These people had only wanted to show appreciation. All of this seemed to me like they were worshiping me. So I told them, as St. Paul had told some people ;many years before, "Get up, I'm not God." And people have asked me saying, "Is it real?" It is so real it hurts.

The Close of the Convention

The next day it was time to "wind up" the convention.

There were all kinds of farewell speeches to be made. It was as though each of the men tried to outdo the other in showing appreciation. So the session got longer and longer, and I wondered if it would ever come to an end. Finally after about four hours it was my turn to speak, and believe me I had no intention of making a long speech, but the people were in no hurry to leave. They weren't going any place. I had received many leis while the farewell speeches were being made. I took a goodly number of the leis from my neck and went over and placed them on Grandma's neck. I called her Grandma Mandapalli. Actually she was the mother of Mrs. Mandapalli, so in that sense she was grandmother of the Mandapalli family.

She Did Not Want to Die Until She Had Seen Me

I should tell you that before I had arrived in India, Grandma Mandapalli had been very sick. In fact, just a week before I had arrived in India, the family had come together for her funeral. In India they bury the body the day after death. They had expected her death. So all of the family had come together for the occasion. They even showed me her coffin which had been prepared for her. The next morning she had sat up on her mat and said, "Is he here yet?" She was referring to me. She did not want to die until she had seen me. And let me tell you for sure she did not miss any part of the convention. That is why I chose to honor her as I did, for ordinarily such a gesture toward a woman would hardly have been considered proper in India. I have more to say about Grandma later, but not now.

The Landlord Requests a Visit

When the convention had come to a close and we were about to break camp, we were invited to visit the landlord at his house. I was told that he wanted to see me. I wondered what we had done that he should be offended. I knew that he was a high caste Hindu for he was the land owner. Not only did he own all the land around the village, but he owned the village. The people who lived in the village all worked for him in the rice fields. They rented a small plot of ground from him, and there they built their homes. The house belonged to the people, but the land belonged to the landlord. So now we were guests at the landlord's house. He set places for all of us on the veranda, and he sat immediately in front of me like he was holding court. I had commended him for his concern for the people of India, for not only did he raise rice, but he also had a large chicken house with some 4000 chickens, so he was also providing other food for the people. Of course, he was also lining his pockets, but I didn't mention that. He was very pleased with the people that had come together that they had created no disturbance in the village. What he really wanted to know was something about the Christian religion. He asked me about our teaching and the teaching of the Catholic church. Since he asked me I was obliged to give him an answer. I told him that we recognize the same God and the same Lord Jesus Christ, and that we believe that Jesus had come into the world to die for our sins. I told him that we do not agree on how we receive what the Lord Jesus has done for us. In the Catholic faith they are taught they must earn or merit what the Lord has done for them, and we believe that we receive what the Lord Jesus has done for us as a free gift, which we receive by faith. I wanted to be as honest with him as I knew how. I did not yet know why he had asked me the question. Finally, he told me that his daughter was attending a Catholic school, and he was interested in knowing something about their teaching. He had been favorably impressed by the people who had come to the convention, so we said we hoped that he, too, might someday become a Christian.

CHAPTER FOUR

Another Mission

On To Visak

The convention had come to a close and I was to spend the next three or four days with Reverend Samuel John of Visakhapatnam. When we went to the train, the Mandapalli family and many of their friends came to the train to see me off. It is so hard to say goodbye to these people because you never know whether you will see them again, but they were already talking about the next time. I shall never forget as the train began to move Naya Mandapalli, the youngest of the Mandapalli family, who had wanted me to bring her back to the States, ran along the train and handed me an apple through the open window. These people really know how to get next to you.

A Visit With Reverend John

Reverent John was to meet me at Visak. He is a Lutheran pastor, born and raised in India, somewhere above Rajahmundry on the Godavari River. He also had received

"The Little Bible of Salvation" about the same time that Peri had received his copy, and he also had translated it into the Telegu language. How fortunate this was for it is his translation that is being used and printed in large print by the Lutheran Braille Workers of California, because Peri's manuscript had been lost in the mail some place between South Dakota and California. How fortunate that we had Reverend John's manuscript as a "back up," so that we could proceed with the publication of the booklet, because the whole mission has come into being and has developed by the use of the booklet.

Back to Rajahmundry

We took the train from Visak back to Rajahmundry. If I had known where Reverend John wanted me to visit, I could have had him come to Rajahmundry and we could have saved a round trip to Rajahmundry. A train ride in India is not the most pleasant experience. It is grimy and dirty, and overcrowded. Sometimes the train stops to chase a cow off the track. That is no joke. You don't run over a cow in India, because the cow might very well have within her the soul of your beloved grandmother. This is part of the pathetic Hindu religion. They believe that the soul of a man returns to animal life after death, and the highest hope for man is that he might become a cow the next time around. That is why they so highly regard the cow. Of course, there is much more to the Hindu religion than this, but this is how it surfaces in the everyday life of the people.

The Blind Leading the Blind

Back to the train trip. It was on one of these rides, either going to Visak or returning to Rajahmundry, that there was a blind beggar on the train. He was being led through the train car asking for alms. There is no way that I can describe the wailing of these two people. I could not help but think of what the Lord Jesus had said about, "The blind leading the blind." But this was the way it was. He was actually being led through the train cars with a rope around his neck. We had been told not to contribute to the beggars in India. I am sure this brought forth a tirade of angry curses as the wailing increased in pitch and tempo. We were told not to give to the beggars because there is no end to it. Besides we would be encouraging this gruesome and vicious industry. Many of the beggars are altogether fake. Many of them have mutilated their own bodies so that the people should have pity on them and give them alms. A person might have chosen to sacrifice his eyes to the gods by looking up at the sun until all vision was gone, and then he might go before the people as a holy man to ask for alms. The people give their gifts with the hope that the "gods" will remember them favorably in the life to come. There is always the hope that the soul might come back in a cow the next time around. The beggar does not say "thank you" when he receives a gift, because he is offering you an opportunity to find favor with the gods. If anything, you are the one that should thank him, that you have had an opportunity to give alms. The worst form of physical abuse is when children have been mutilated by their own parents. With broken arms, and broken legs, or even with broken backs, they drag themselves through the streets asking for alms. The "take" all belongs to the family. Sometimes children fall into the hands of some scoundrel who has similarly mutilated the bodies of the children. Then he sends them out on the streets to beg. They turn over the loot at the end of the day. Some of these scoundrels have many such children working the streets for them and they become fabulously rich.

Call a Taxi

When we arrived in Rajahmundry it was necessary for us

to contact a taxi driver to take us on a trip up the Godavari river to the Polavaram valley. This is the valley where Reverend John was born and raised. At one time there had been many Lutheran churches in this area, but now there was only one missionary. When we contacted a taxi driver, immediately he began to hassle about the price. The taxi driver wanted 200 rupees for his services. Pastor John came to me and told me that that was too much. Finally we agreed on 175 rupees with no "extra benefits" along the way.

A Hospitable Hostel

Before we left Rajahmundry we stopped at a hostel, which was owned by the Lutheran church of Andhra Pradesh. At one time there had been a very active church in this part of India. Reverend John told me that it had been a mission of the Evangelical Lutheran Church of Germany. But during World War II when the British and Germans were at war, the mission was turned over to the United Lutheran Church in America, now known as the L.C.A. However, the L.C.A. did not do much to support the native ministry. As a result, many of the pastors serving in that area had to take up other work to survive, and the ministry was quite forsaken. As a result, the hostel was scarcely used at all. Here we had a meal, which of course, I provided. Then we were on our way.

Keeping Tab

We hadn't gone very far when we had to stop for gas. Of course, I had to buy the gas. We went over a bridge and I had to pay the toll. Almost immediately after we crossed the bridge we had to stop for oil. They never seem to buy gas and oil at the same stop. Further down the road we had to stop for more gas. I think they buy only one gallon of gas at a time. I kept track of all that I had to pay out, for we had agreed that there would be no extras, and I would have to pay the difference at the end of the trip.

Down by the Riverside

Toward evening, we arrived at a village where I preached to a group of people down by the river. After the service, Pastor John told me that there were a number of people who would like for me to baptize them. Well, there was a whole river of water so that should be no problem. I didn't know whether I should step out into the water to baptize the people, or have the water brought up from the river for the baptism. I chose to have the water brought up for the baptism. These were people who had been prepared for baptism by Reverend Samuel John. It was about dark, but we were scheduled to speak at another village that night, so we drove to the next village. As we drove to this village we had to pass through another small village on the way. It so happened that a chicken decided to cross the road, but it didn't make it. Immediately a crowd of people gathered and waved angry fists as us as we drove off. The taxi driver had committed a serious crime. He had run over someone's chicken.

A Worship Service on the Street

We drove on and on, what seemed to be an endless trip. It was pitch dark and the road seemed to have come to an end long ago. Finally we came to the village where I had been scheduled to preach. We were an hour or two late, but the people were waiting for us. There we had a church service in the street. There were no street lights. So we had a service in the dark, with no light but the burning torches. I had a flash light which gave me some light so I could conduct the service. After the service, which was all interpreted by Reverend John, the people asked to be baptized. Thus we had a baptism on the street. After baptizing some of the parents, some of them wanted me to baptize their children, also. I baptized two children of one family, a little boy and a little girl. I suppose they were two or three years old. Neither one of them had any clothes on. The little girl had a string around her waist and a fig-leaf pendant in front to indicate that this was a girl. Also that evening a mother brought a child to be baptized after she had been baptized. She was holding the child in her arms. As she turned the child around to face me, the child screamed and kicked until it broke away from his mother. The poor child had never seen a white person, and sure enough, he thought he had seen a ghost. The lady ran out in the darkness, found the child and brought him back for baptism. I don't know how she ever found him. It was so dark that I couldn't see any of the people ten feet away.

And Yet Another Service

We drove on. I thought the day was far spent. But I was to speak at yet another church in another village. The people had almost given up hope of us getting there that night. But when we arrived, word was passed along, and soon the people had gathered at the church, although it was now three hours after they had expected us to be there.

Rest for the Weary

Finally the day was done and we stayed in a hostel which was maintained in the village for out-of-town guests and government officials. Here was an opportunity to rest and be refreshed, and have a good meal that was brought in. The next day, after breakfast we went on up the river to another village. We drove as far as we could. Then we walked into the village where again I was to speak to the people.

Beyond Civilization

We were now quite far from civilization, and the people were very shy. Only the men came to the service, which was conducted on the street between two dung heaps. This time the service was being translated into Koya, one of the dialect languages. I do not know for sure if the Bible has ever been translated into Koya, but Reverend John's sister had seen to it that the "Little Bible of Salvation" was translated into Koya. We were in the valley where Reverend John had been born and raised by his missionary father. As I mentioned before, there had been fourteen Lutheran churches in the valley, but now there was only one young man striving to revive the churches. I mentioned that the women did not come to the service. They stood at a distance outside of their huts, in back of trees to see what was going on. After the service Reverend John told me that I was to pray for the sick, but nobody came. I asked if I should pray for all the sick in general, and let it go at that. He said, "No, they will come." And sure enough, they came. One woman stood before me with a child in her arms. I am not a doctor, but it did not take a physician to know that she was burning up with fever, and her child also had the fever. I was quite sure she had malaria. I prayed for them. Soon another lady came carrying a child that had some ugly ulcers on its body. I don't know what it was, but was quite sure that this was leprosy. I prayed for her and the child and then I said, "Lord, what these people need is medicine." I talked with Pastor John about the need for medical help. He assured me that they do have free medical help in India. But the problem is that these people live so far away from the clinic. There is no means of transportation in the hill country. These people cannot afford to hire someone to take them to a doctor. So many of the people do not receive medical help.

Retracing Our Steps

It was mid-morning and now we began our return trip to Rajahmundry. We followed the same routine of stopping for gas and oil. When we came to the village where we had run over the chicken the night before the people barricaded the road. They knew we would be coming back because there was no other road. They continued to rant and rave about the dead chicken which they held up by the neck to show us and to make us fell guilty. I do not know how the taxi driver settled the matter, but finally they cleared the road and let us go on our way.

The Hospice Centre

After several more pit stops for gas and oil we arrived at the hostel at Rajahmundry. And again we were to stay for a meal. It was good to find such hospitality in India even if I had to provide the meal. I wish that we could secure this particular property for our mission, because it is not being used very well as a hospice centre, since the need for a hospice centre no longer exists. There is about an acre and a half of land on the water front facing the Godavari River. Otherwise the compound is completely enclosed with a high wall. The hospice home was a very substantial building, very suitable for the lifestyle of India. Here an orphanage, a care home for the aged, a Bible Centre and a school for children could be located. This would be an ideal place from which to conduct our mission. "Oh well, it's all right to dream."

Time for Reckoning

We had a train to catch, so we went out to the taxi. By this time I had figured out that the taxi driver intended to charge me 175 rupees although I had already paid him 145 rupees for all the extras. I anticipated we would have some difficulties when we got to the train station. So I went to the back of the taxi and wrote down the license number of the taxi. Sure enough, when it came time to make payment he wanted 175 rupees. I told him that he had agreed to drive for 175 rupees with no extras. I offered him 35 rupees. He would not accept them. Since we had agreed on the terms the day before, I told him, "I have written down the number of your taxi, and I will report you to the American consulate. They will take it up with the Indian government, and you will stand to lose your license." By this time a large group of people had gathered round and were yakking at him. Finally, Reverend John said, "Offer him 40 rupees." This I did and he accepted it. When he had gone, I asked Reverend John what it was that the people had said to him. He said, "They told him to accept the money and be on his way before he got into trouble."

Visak and Reformation Service

Soon the train arrived and we were involved in a mad scramble to get on the train, which can be quite an ordeal in itself as the train is nearly a mile long. We had been assigned to a certain seat in one of the coaches, but we were not sure which coach was ours.

Here let me retrace my steps a bit. When I first arrived in Visak I had become quite sick with Delhi Belly. I had stopped at the office of Air India to rearrange some details concerning my return trip. I wanted to be sure that I had flight reservations, so that I could meet a certain flight at Bombay. While I was at the office of Air India I made a quick stop at the bathroom. There I left my camera hanging on the wall. I was so sick that I did not realize that I had left it. We made the trip up the Godavari River not knowing what had become of the camera. Of course, I could not take any pictures.

But now that we were back at Visak I was to preach at the Lutheran church at Makkuva on the outskirts of Visak. It was Friday evening, October 31. I was to preach a Reformation sermon. I was desperately sick. I have never preached with such pain in my stomach. It felt as though there was a "sword fight" in my innards. They had hired some special musicians for the occasion. What music! I wish that I had recorded the music. The drummer tapped out the music on the bongo drums with such precise rhythm as I have never heard anywhere else. He outdid himself in that the beautiful voices of the girls who sang were subdued by the drums. It was a Reformation service that I shall never forget. I was to return to preach on Sunday.

The Lost is Found

The next morning being Saturday, I was to speak at an interdenominational ministerial gathering to tell them about India Bible League and Project Philip. On the way to this gathering we went back to Air India's office. I had determined that I had not seen the camera since I had stopped there a few days earlier. Sure enough, they had my camera, but I would have to wait until the proper officials arrived to release it. They wanted me to appreciate that the camera was being returned to me. They did not want a reward. They just wanted me to be sure to put in a "good word" with the officials of Air India. Indeed, I wrote to the officials to tell them about the faithfulness of their officers. I was very glad to get the camera again, for you see it was not really my camera. It belonged to our son, Philip. He had loaned it to me and I knew I would be unable to replace it.

A Christian Funeral Service

After I received the camera we proceeded to the meeting of the pastors. The representative of India Bible League had not arrived from Madras. So I did the best that I could to tell them about India Bible League, and their desire to get the Bible to all the people of India. They want to use all of the church groups of India to help them with distribution of the Bibles. The meeting was cut short because there was a funeral at the Lutheran church in downtown Visak. A prominent lady of the church had passed away on Friday, so the funeral had to be held on Saturday. They do not embalm the bodies of the dead in India. Pastor John and I attended the funeral. This was a unique experience. Various people came to the casket and presented wreaths or leis of flowers, and offered their eulogies. The pastor also had a sermon. Most of the service was in Telegu, although occasionally some English was spoken. The service lasted for two hours or more. No one is in a hurry in India.

Outside of the church stood a funeral coach, a small carriage decked in black, drawn by a small black horse, which stood there unattended all through the service. It seems the animals are as well disciplined as the children of India. They simply do what they are supposed to do. It is certainly a different world. I might mention here that Christian people usually bury the bodies in India. The Hindu people usually burn the bodies, and the Sikhs place the bodies on pyres and let the vultures devour them.

A Traditional Lutheran Church Service

We returned to the hotel where I was able to rest up for the service on Sunday. This was a very traditional Lutheran church service. The men sat on one side of the church during the service, and the women sat on the other side. It was as though I was worshiping in one of our Lutheran churches forty or fifty years ago. The only thing different about the sermon was that Reverend John stood by me and interpreted the sermon as I preached. I thought to myself, "How wonderful it would be if we always had someone standing by us in the pulpit telling the people what we were trying to say." Really it is a thrilling experience to preach in this way. After the preaching they had Holy Communion. I do not know whether they had grape juice or wine. I do know that Reverend John had a flask of water and diluted the wine or grape juice, because it was so thick that it would hardly flow from the bottle. Oh yes, we also had a baptism and a confirmation. I was to baptize a young man who had been prepared for membership and Pastor John confirmed him.

I almost forgot to mention the special offering for the communion. This was a practice that once existed in many of the Lutheran churches years ago, but has generally been discontinued because we do not want the people to think that they can buy the forgiveness of sins at the altar. However, these people were being taught that their gift was a "love offering." It was so inscribed on the silver offering tray that was used. I also noticed that the young man reached into his pocket to give an offering when he was confirmed. Some people had come to the altar with special requests for prayers and they too gave a "thank offering." Anyhow, this was the way it was done at the Lutheran church in Makkuva near Visak. It is not all bad because one of the major concerns is to teach these people to share their blessings with the Lord, lest they become "rice Christians" and their Christianity fade away when they no longer receive gifts of rice. It certainly was not out of place that these people be given a chance to present love offerings or thank offerings.

Return to the States

The next day I was to begin my trip back to the States, and now I was alone. Up to this point I had depended upon someone else to make arrangements for me, and to do whatever hassling had to be done. Now I was to pay the coolie for carrying my luggage, and for helping me to get to the right line at the ticket office, and to get me on the right plane at take-off time. Of course, we also had to go through customs every time that we had to board a plane. How glad I would be when all this was over. My last cab ride was to the airport in Bombay where a coolie met me to help with my luggage. I had paid two rupees wherever we went in India for such service, but now, when I was leaving India and offered the usual two rupees, the coolie suddenly wanted 20 rupees. After some haggling, I finally gave him the 20 rupees, mainly because we could not take any Indian money with us when we left the country. We would be required to exchange it for our own currency before we left. So it turned out that I didn't have much money to exchange.

Finally we were in the plane and "air borne." How good it was to not have to hassle anymore about prices! I made a mental note that I must remember to write all of the pastors who had been praying for me, which I did as soon as I arrived home. I was tired and tried to sleep, but I kept waking at twelve o'clock thinking it was time to get up. What a terrible jet-lag. I couldn't go back to sleep because I kept reliving all the things that had happened to me on this most memorable occasion of my life.

But lest you think that this is the end of the story, let me tell you that this is just the beginning.

CHAPTER FIVE

How the Mission Developed (1979-1983)

First Things First

When I got back home I took care of what pastoral responsibilities I had to take care of. Then I went to Chadron, Nebraska to get Arda. She had spent the time with friends and relatives. We began immediately to tell people about the mission at every opportunity. We contacted Lawrence and Mildred Petrosky at Wessington Springs, South Dakota. Mildred had asked me if I might find some child that they might support. I told them about the little girl who had been wandering about during the convention, and staying with anybody who would take her home with them. Her lovely smile had won for her many a meal. She had learned that her smile got things for her. Otherwise we did not often see the children smile. Most of them did not have much for which they could be happy. The little girl's name is Rajeswari. They gladly accepted the responsibility of this child. She was the first child to receive support. Gradually we told people about the mission and the orphans, and in due time we had support for the thirty orphans at Kesavaram. The first thing I told the ladies of our church at Wessington Springs, South Dakota, was, "Make some blankets about 3 feet by 5 feet so that the children in the orphanage might have something to sleep on." The children slept on dirt floors without any covering. Very shortly we had blankets for all of these children.

Additional Support

I took a month off from my parish ministry during the summer and traveled. I spoke to the people wherever I had an opportunity. We found people were most anxious to support this kind of ministry, because they knew that the money that they were giving would actually be used for the purpose for which it was given. We traveled 4,350 miles during the month of August and I spoke at 30 different gatherings of people.

A Gift With a Purpose

The young people of St. John's Lutheran Church of St. James, Minnesota gave me a gift of $100. I hardly knew how to say thanks because this was so unexpected. I told the young people, "Your gift will be used to buy a bicycle for our mission." I knew that they could use a bicycle at the mission. Little did I realize how important this gift would turn out to be. Our bicycle evangelist took 200 of the "Little Bible of Salvation" booklets, which had been provided for us by the Lutheran Braille workers in the Telegu language. He peddled his way into the village of PeddiPalem. There he distributed the booklets. So far as anyone knows, there had never been an evangelist of any kind in this village. He did not hold a preaching service. He just distributed the booklet. A few days later, the people of the village came to our director, Peri Sastry Mandapalli, and asked him to come to their village and

preach for them. One hundred and fifty people showed up for the first service. Then the people asked Peri to send them an evangelist to teach them how to become Christian. Now everyone knows that the Hindu people would not do something like that, but they did. Peri wrote to me and asked, "Pastor Daddy, what do I do?" I wrote back to him and said, "Send them an evangelist." So we began with our first full-time evangelist in a village where there had never been an evangelist before. That was only the beginning. Shortly thereafter, they had established an orphanage, so we had another 40 children to take care of. I mention this story not only because it is most unusual, but also to indicate that something is happening in India today. And the people are beginning to say, "What about Christianity?"

The Mandapalli Family Carries On With the Mission

Peri's brother, John, soon got involved and he established an orphanage for 20 children. By now we had 90 orphans and gradually we secured support for the most of these children. I saw that Peri would soon be involved with more responsibilities than he could handle, so I appointed Ammaji, his oldest sister, to help supervise the orphanage work. She was to get $1.00 for each child she was supervising and when she was getting $30.00 per month, she was to ask someone to help her. We had deliberately set $30.00 as the maximum support that would be granted to any of the workers. It was not long before she had to ask for help, so she asked Naya, her younger sister, to help her until she was receiving $30.00 a month, and then she asked her sister-in-law to help. It might strike you as most unusual that all of the members of the Mandapalli family would be involved in this mission. The story behind all of this is that their father had been an evangelist. He had done much preaching and had baptized many people in the area, but now he had passed away. The children of the family all wanted to carry on with the same ministry as their father had done. Surely they would do this to honor the Lord Jesus, but also no doubt, it was because their father had been an evangelist. In India you do what your father has done.

The older members of the family all had received a university education. Proudly they told me that Ammaji had received a double degree in education. Which means that she could teach almost anywhere in India, but she prefers to work with the mission. Naya had been studying to become a nurse, but she had not completed her education when her father died. So her education had been terminated. She wanted me to adopt her and take her to America so she could complete her education. But that was not possible. We have tried for several years to get Ammaji to come to America to live with us so that she might tell firsthand about the mission in Kesavaram. We just haven't been able to get visa clearance for her.

Frieda Hanson Lends Her Support

I must tell you about a lady who lives in South Dakota, who had heard about the mission in Kesavaram. Her name is Frieda Hanson. She lives with her husband, Joe, in Madison, South Dakota. She had become interested in mission work in India several years before, and had gone to India to visit. When she heard about our work in India she made another trip to India in the spring of 1981. She took some pictures of the children at the orphanage. I cried when I saw the pictures. I knew these children from my first visit to India. How much better they looked, now that they were receiving better food. Mrs. Hanson also provided new clothes for all of the children.

She is a wonderful lady, and dearly loves the people of India. She has encouraged and admonished us to provide a better home for the children. She says, "It is not right that the children should live in such crowded conditions. We must find a better place for them to live." As I write these memoirs I can say that negotiations are underway to relocate the orphanage at Rejahmundry and purchase a building there. Most of the money has been made available for the purchase of this property. Much of the money was given by the people of India who appreciate what our director is doing for the children in India. We still need to complete the transaction.

Support Increases

Here let me mention that support for the mission has continued to grow from year to year. In 1977 our total receipts were $1,254. In 1983 the total receipts were $18,793. All of the finances flow through "The Little Bible of Salvation Foundation" which is a tax deductible organization registered in the state of Oklahoma. Most of the gifts are designated for a specific orphan or for a certain evangelist or Bible woman. All designated gifts are sent directly to India and used as designated. People receive correspondence from India, reassuring them that the money they have given is being used as intended. This is very important so that we establish a trustworthy accountability for all of the gifts which we receive. So far we have not lost any money which has been sent to India. All checks of any size are sent by registered mail. One letter arrived in India without any contents, so we sent a notice to the bank to stop payment in case that the check should be found and someone would try to cash it. We have lost some parcels which were sent by airmail. It seems that such items which require import duty present a special temptation, and they become more susceptible to confiscation.

Gifts of Clothing

We have sent many boxes of used clothing every year. So far as we know they have all arrived at the proper destination, although it takes from four to six months before they get to India. You cannot imagine the requests that we get from the people asking us to send used clothing. Every day we receive letters from India and almost always they ask for used clothing. About half of the children in India under twelve years of age run around without any clothes. They would wear clothes if they had them. Somehow we must find a way to get parcels of clothing to these people. It doesn't make any sense to send them to us, and that we in turn should send them to India, although this we would do. Perhaps if anyone would like to help with such a venture we could give the names and addresses of people who could receive such gifts and distribute them to the poor.

Some might say we give our gifts through World Relief. This is all good and well, but it doesn't reach people such as these. A few years ago it was reported that our Lutheran ladies had contributed 100,000 blankets for World Relief, and that they were all sent to India. It was also mentioned that Sister Theresa had received 100,000 blankets and distributed them in Calcutta. Presumably they were the same blankets. This is very commendable and certainly we would not begrudge anyone who received a blanket. I mentioned at a meeting that it was not possible for our mission to receive any of these blankets. The person who was speaking was very much offended that I would make such a statement. She assured me that the blankets were available for anyone. However, I checked into this later, and sure enough, it is not possible for our mission to receive any such help. Our mission is not yet recognized as an established church group in that part of India. Sending the gift directly is the only sure way that there is to get the gift to the people whom you wish to help. And believe me, these people are very happy when they receive such gifts.

Retirement

The mission continued to grow month by month, and week by week, as more and more evangelists and Bible women became acquainted with our mission. They began using "The Little Bible of Salvation" in their witness, and they report that many people are becoming Christians by the use of this booklet. Support for the mission and for the orphans also continued to increase, as I had opportunity to speak and tell our people about the mission. I decided to retire from the active ministry so that I would have more time to promote the mission. I had reached the magic age of retirement. I could retire and collect social security, and pension, and receive a greater income than I was receiving in the ministry. And besides, such income was tax deductible, as indeed it should be, because we had already paid our social security tax for 40 years and paid taxes on our income for as many years. It was like getting a raise in salary simply because we did not have to pay income tax on our social security and pension. I accepted a call to serve as assistant pastor at Immanuel Lutheran Church in Springfield, Illinois. At that time we were allowed to work 20 hours a week and earn up to $5,500 a year which was also tax deductible. The salary I received from Immanuel was actually the only money that we were earning, as the social security and pension is simply money which we now receive which had been withheld from our salary for some 40 years. Now at least we could pay our bills.

Part-time Ministry

The arrangement of working for Immanuel 20 hours a week gave me much more time to promote the mission in India. I had much more opportunity to speak at the various churches about our mission in India. We had hoped that Ammaji Mandapalli would be able to come and live with us for a year or more. But this did not work out as she could not get visa clearance. We also had hoped that our director, Peri Sastry, would be able to come to America to attend one of our seminaries to prepare himself to be one of our missionaries. Such an agreement had been made by officials of the church in St. Louis, but this did not materialize either. It was required of Peri that he take certain theological courses by correspondence. All of this has taken time. He completed two of the courses and did very well, but he never got around to completing the third course. There is no question that as the work developed in India he found less and less time to work on his lessons.

How is it Going?

After a period of four years I decided that it was time to visit the mission again to see how things were going. One of my chief concerns has been to keep all of the evangelists working together, lest they go off in as many directions as there were evangelists. They were all independent evangelists, and nobody was responsible to anyone else but me. And I was living 12,000 miles away on the other side of the world. It had been four years since I had been there. Yes, we would go to India. This time I would take Arda, my wife, along with me. So we sold a lot that we had purchased some years earlier out in Arizona, and financed the trip. There was no way that we would take money from the foundation for the trip, although the trip was being made in behalf on the mission. Neither did we have $6,000 lying around waiting to be spent. So we sold the lot, and we were off on our second honeymoon. We though we would take our second honeymoon even now though it was 40 years later.

CHAPTER SIX

Our Second Visit to Kesavaram

Don't Come Now

If you will, we would invite you to make this second trip with us and see the mission through two pairs of eyes. Our visit to India had been planned for the month of August 1983. We received word that we should not come in August because August is the month of the monsoons. Sure enough, they had very heavy rains and floods in August. So we were rescheduled to leave for India in October. And wouldn't you know, they even had worse floods in October than they had in August.

Pastor Kaufmann's father and mother had been in Springfield for a visit. Pastor Kaufmann is the pastor at Immanuel Lutheran Church in Springfield. His parents took us to Chicago to catch our flight to India. We left Chicago on October 23 and arrived in New Delhi on October 25th. That is a long time to be up in the air, but I was used to being up in the air after 40 years of marriage.

Friends Visit India

Friends from western Kansas by the name of Don and Cleone Neff were going to meet us in India. They were not on the same flight with us. Mrs. Neff was born and raised in India. Her father, Rev. Paul Kaufeldt, had been a missionary in India years ago. She had not been back to visit India since she had left India 41 years earlier. Her interest was to visit in Kerala State where she had lived as a child, but they wanted to visit our mission in Kesavaram also.

Welcome to India

Peri and Rao, one of the evangelists from Visakhapatnam, met us in New Delhi. We had made arrangements to visit the Tajmahal. Some friends of ours, Eugene and Esther Staska of Chadron, Nebraska, had planned on making the trip with us. They had to cancel out because Eugene had a bad back. He could never have survived the trip to India, at least not this part of the trip. Peri and his friend had not seen the Taj, and, of course, Arda had not seen it either, so our first day was spent in a taxi driving over to Agra to see the Taj. Everyone must see the Taj when they visit India. I had seen it four years before when I was in India. It was as magnificent as ever. Peri and Arda enjoyed taking pictures of the Taj and other things.

Patty Cake, Patty Cake

Arda could even tell you how the women in India gather the fresh cow dung and make pancakes and plaster them on the walls of the buildings to dry. Each cake has the hand imprint of the woman who plastered it to the wall. When these patty cakes are dried they are gathered and placed in a dry shelter. This is one of the chief sources of fuel used for cooking in India.

What Can a Body Endure?

We returned to Delhi in the evening. I don't know when I have ever been so tired, and our trip was really just beginning. We had a good rest at the YMCA. Arrangements had been made for us to stay at the "Y". These were reasonable accommodations. They even served us our meals. We had been cautioned again and again not to eat any fresh fruits or vegetables. We had a bacon and tomato sandwich at the "Y", and sure enough, in no time I was getting queasy.

The next day we were to board a train and travel to Rajahmundry. This was an endurance contest. We traveled for 27 hours. When night came we folded up the back of the seat to make a cot overhead so we had a double-decker sleeper. The cushions were about as soft as a plank. It was because of this part of our trip that I said, "The Staskas could not have survived." We were not prepared for the cold night. I did not realize that it can be cold at night at that time of the year, although I knew right well the frost was on the pumpkin back home in Illinois. Peri, however, had brought a couple of blankets which he shared with us. Imagine how surprised I was in the morning when I discovered that these were surely the same blankets that I had sewn together when we were living in South Dakota. "Let nothing be lost." They can make good use of small blankets made of any kind of scrap materials. Most of the people in India simply lie down to sleep on the dirt floor without any blanket to sleep on. Neither do they have one to cover them at night. I suppose they could use 600,000,000 blankets in India, but most of the people could not afford to buy one even if they were available.

They Wish Us Well

A friend of Peri's had met us at the train station in New Delhi. He was a Lutheran minister's son attending a university at New Delhi. His mother had prepared a lunch for us to eat on the train, although we had our own survival food with us. Everything tasted very good because we were getting hungry. She had sent some bananas and oranges which are safe to eat, and there were some of the most beautiful luscious grapes that I had ever seen. Arda warned me not to eat the grapes. I resisted for a long time, but after 18 or 20 hours on the train I couldn't resist any longer. It wasn't long before I was put in mind of the fact that Eve gave some fruit that she had picked in the garden of Eden to Adam, and he ate it. The Lord God had said, "If you eat of it, you will surely die." It really began to churn in my stomach. Already I had the Delhi-belly, and it was to last for two months. Fortunately I was able to keep it subdued because I had taken a water distiller along with us and we either boiled or distilled all of our drinking water. This gave us much relief.

Destination

Then we came to Rajahmundry area, the train moved very slowly along the track. The roadbed had been saturated by the flood waters which had been over the railroad track a few days earlier. One could see the debris hanging from the top of the telegraph poles along the track. Surely the water had been 15 feet deep along the track. This had been a terrible flood. Hundreds of thousands of acres of land had been under water, and hundreds of thousands of people had lost their homes. Even the rice which grows in the rice paddies could not put up with that amount of water. So there was very little harvest. If any of the rice was harvested it was not quality rice. The train stopped at every little village and the people gathered along the track and came up and looked in the train windows. Most of these people had never seen a white man and surely not a white woman. Sometimes you wake up at night and see those big brown eyes looking at you. You never forget them.

Better Late Than Never

When we arrived at Rajahmundry many of the people had come to the train to meet us. We were only three hours late, but they are accustomed to waiting in India. We were transported to our hotel at Tanuka by bicycle rickshaws. There were five in number because we had been joined by a number of friends, who had met us at the train station to bid us welcome. It was quite a caravan as we traveled through the streets to the hotel. We stayed in the same hotel in which I had stayed four years earlier, when I visited the mission the first time, although the convention was being held at a different village this time.

On to the Convention

It was Sunday morning. We were joined by the Neffs from Kansas, who had come to be with us for the opening of the second convention. They had traveled by taxi to get there. How they knew where to find us I will never know. But Cleone had been raised in India and she knew very well how to get around. We drove by taxi to the convention centre at Tadeparru. Peri had rented a tent for the occasion. When we came to the edge of the village crowds of people lined the streets to welcome us. Finally the taxi stopped and we walked the last six blocks to the convention centre. A four piece band had been hired for the occasion. They went before us and played various religious songs. If the people knew the songs they joined in singing. Anyone who knew me, and had met me when I had visited four years earlier, came out of the crowds that lined the streets and held me by the arm. As we marched along I envisioned that we were marching right up to heaven. I remembered a song that my father used to sing to us when we were little children. "We're marching to Zion, beautiful, beautiful Zion. We're marching upward to Zion, the beautiful city of God." Surely this was a group of Christians

marching right up to heaven. The little girl who had stood by
me and fanned me in my room when I visited India the first
time came out of the crowd and held me by the arm. She
didn't let go until we were at the convention centre. She is a
lovely girl. She is shown in a picture here. I will say more
about her later.

What a Welcome

Welcome banners hung across the street to welcome each
family. One for us, and one for the Neffs and one for the
Staskas, who did not get to make the trip. Pictures were taken
from time to time throughout the service. Welcome speeches
were made by Peri and his brother John and others. Ammaji
and Naya Mandapalli led the assembly in singing. How the
people love to sing. Much of their theology is learned by
singing. Most of it was in Telegu, but some singing was in
English. They even had a lovely "Velkom" song. I was to
preach the sermon, and Peri was to translate for me. In back
of us hung a white sheet with a ribbon across the front of it.
Arda was to cut the ribbon at a given time to reveal a picture
of me. An artist had painted the picture from a black and
white photo that was several years old. The artist had done a
remarkably good job, considering what he had to work with.
He used good color. He gave me distinctive blue eyes, and
even restored a considerable amount of my hair. I should have
given him a special tip for that.

Recognition Time

Certificates of membership had been prepared for all of the
evangelists and Bible women who had registered. We were
told that there were 125 evangelists and 40 Bible women who
attended the convention. On one of the days during the
convention I was to meet each of the evangelists and the Bible
women individually. We took pictures of each of them. I have

not been able to identify all of them. It was just more than I could handle. For rest and relaxation we were to stay in the home of one of the leading men of the community. He was probably the owner of the village. He was a Hindu of high caste. It was a very lovely home with ample accommodations. I wished that we had been permitted to stay at their home,

rather than commute to the hotel for the night. This man was very accommodating. He apologized for his children who were curious and would sneak a look at us whenever they could. He said, "You must forgive the children. They have never seen a white person before." We had a camera with us that would take a picture which would develop in two minutes. We took pictures of the children and gave them to the children. When others learned about this they also wanted their pictures taken. It was truly like magic for them to be able to see a picture develop before their eyes.

Her Name is Arda

One day at the convention, a lady stood in the back of the
crowd and waved her hand at us and pointed to the baby that
she was holding. She lifted the child up so that we could see
her. I knew immediately who this was although I had never
seen the lady. A year earlier a pastor had written to me and
asked me to suggest a name for his granddaughter. This I did
not do. A few months later he wrote to me that he had

baptized his granddaughter, and that he had given her the
name of "Arda." I had sent them a small gift of money that
they should celebrate the child's first birthday. This they had
done. It happens to be on the same day as our oldest
daughter's birthday. We had to take a picture to give to them
and take one for ourselves. One can sure spend a fortune on
that kind of photography. The lady wanted that my wife
should hold her little granddaughter. They have a way of

60

becoming part of your family. But little Arda would have nothing to do with her "grandmother Arda," for she had never seen a white person. I predict that in a very few years there will be many little girls in India with the name of Arda. And there is no way that Arda can be grandmother to all of them.

An Exercise in Religious Futility

One morning just as we were getting into our taxi to go out to the convention centre, a young lad, a boy about fourteen or fifteen years of age, approached the cab. He had a machete sticking through his throat back of the windpipe. Seemingly blood was streaming down the sides of his neck. Of course, he was asking for alms. Now whether this was for real, or whether it was all fake, I was not able to discern. I called it an exercise in religious futility. If it was real, if he actually had a machete struck through his throat, then he had performed this act as a personal sacrifice to the gods in order that he might present himself as an object of pity before the people, so that they might perform their alms. If it was fake, and indeed it might have been, then he was only out to get the alms from the people by deceiving them. Then he was most certainly also offending the gods. I talked with a knowledgeable person in India about this and he said it was probably real and it might have been performed as an act of devil worship which is also found in India.

Lord, Send a Helicopter

All did not go as we had intended at the convention, for I had become very sick with the Delhi-belly. On the third day of the convention I did not attend the sessions at all. I stayed in the hotel room all day trying to recuperate so that I could carry on the next day. I was so sick I wanted to go home, but I was in no shape to make such a trip. I said, "Lord, send a helicopter and take me out of this place. I don't want to die in

India. I don't care what you do with Arda, but get me out of here." Well, sometimes the Lord doesn't listen to your prayers, because He has more important things to do.

They Care

The Mandapalli family came to visit at the hotel and stayed all afternoon. I believe it was Ammaji's birthday. Anyhow, we celebrated her birthday while we were there. I had my tape recorder in the room so I asked the girls to sing some songs which I taped. Sujaya Mandapalli, John's oldest daughter, who had given me such a special welcome, sat on my bed and decided she would teach me to sing Telegu. We turned on the recorder and she got real close to my face, and as she sang it was almost as though she formed the words in my mouth. I was to repeat each phrase after her. So we recorded a song. I have no idea what the words meant, but the family was very happy that I now could sing in Telegu. I told them that Sujaya should grow up to be a linguist, because she was very capable and very persistent in teaching me. She handles both languages quite well.

Oliver, John's oldest son, was also in the room with us. He has been receiving support from Mr. and Mrs. Leon Seebeck of Verdon, Oklahoma. I told them when they selected his picture that he was not an orphan, but if they chose to give him support it would be applied to his education, and without doubt he would become one of the leaders in our mission in the next generation. Already he has been attending special school so he can handle English. He has already decided that he will be an evangelist and work with the mission. He sat in our room and wrote a letter to his sponsors in Oklahoma.

The girls stayed in the room all afternoon, also. Naya, who had had some training as a nurse, had a thermometer and took my temperature. She also fixed some citrus drink that I should take. John's wife, Salomi, and Ammaji were also there. With such beautiful girls in the room I could not help but feel better, and I forgot all about the helicopter, which I had asked the Lord to send. I was on cloud nine and didn't need a helicopter. I was getting better fast.

"I Pray For You"

When the older members of the family had left the room the three younger daughters of John Mandapalli stayed in the room. Sujaya, the oldest of the girls, said, "I pray for you." Then she knelt down by my bed and prayed a long, long prayer. The kind that some of our pastors used to pray when I was a small child and I wondered if they would ever get done. When she had finished her prayer, the next girl said, "I pray for you." She also prayed a long, long prayer, in Telegu, of course. I reckon that the Lord understands Telegu as well as English. When she had finished the youngest of the girls said, "I pray for you." And she prayed a long, long prayer. I am sure the Lord heard their prayers because I felt much better the next day.

I mention this little episode to give you some concept of the quality of Christianity that exists in India. These little girls are third generation Christians. Where in all this would would you find three little girls that would thus voluntarily kneel down and pray at the bedside of a stranger, or anyone for that matter.

Visiting the People

On the following day I was recuperated enough so that I could get on with visiting the people and attending the meetings. We decided to visit Dr. and Mrs. Arthur living at Chettapeta in Nidadvole. Here the doctor is ministering to the needs of the people. He works mostly among the lepers and the very poor people. He receives very little for his services, as most of these people cannot afford to pay anything. I wish

you could all meet this man and his wife. For that reason I
have included a couple of pictures. The doctor is taking care
of a leper patient. Mrs. Arthur is presenting a small blanket to
one of the orphan children. There is no way that we can
describe how happy these people are to receive such gifts as a
small blanket three feet by five feet made of scraps of used
clothing sewn together..

Dr. Arthur distributes "The Little Bible of Salvation"
regularly to his patients, and establishes a good Christian
witness. Mrs. Arthur, Santhi Arthur, maintains an orphanage
for 12 children and does evangelistic work as a Bible woman
wherever possible. We decided to visit the Arthurs. We got
into a taxi, and were on our way. And when I say we got into
the taxi that means that as many as could possibly get into the
taxi went along. It all costs the same whether there is one
person or whether there are eight or ten people in the cab.

No Road

We drove for some time. The roads were very bad because
of the recent floods. We got within five miles of the village
where Dr. and Mrs. Arthur live. The roads were washed out
and the canal ditch next to the road had also been washed out
by the flood. We stopped at a village which had been
completely inundated by the flood. Some houses were still
standing, but they would eventually come tumbling down,
because the mud brick walls had been thoroughly saturated.
We visited with the people of the village, but could not get
any definite information as to how we might find the Arthurs.
It seemed we had made the trip in vain.

Another Child to Support

While Peri was visiting with the people he met a lady who
had lost her husband in an accident shortly before the flood,
and now she had lost everything she had in the flood. She

64

wanted to become a Bible woman and work with our mission.
She had a daughter about 11 years old. Peri promised to take
her into one of the orphanages. I promised that we would find
a sponsor to provide a minimum of $10.00 a month to hep
take care of her. When we got back to the States she was the

first one for whom we secured a sponsor. Her name is Baby
Kumari. And now her sponsors will know that we mentioned
her by name in our book. The name Baby does not mean
"baby" as you might think. As near as I could tell, it was
pronounced "bobby," like short for Roberta. At least that is
what her name sounds like in Indian English. I instructed Peri
to leave the girl with her mother rather than to take her to the
already overcrowded orphanage. In that way the mother
would also have something to eat, and she would still have
the responsibility of taking care of her daughter. We did not
get to visit the Arthurs at their home. However, Dr. Arthur
visited us in our hotel room the next day. He is absolutely a
gem. There are not many people like him in this world. After
I got back home I sent my water distiller to Dr. Arthur for him
to use in his medical practice in India. I have learned more
recently that the doctor has been contacted by the Swedish
mission society who is working together with the Indian
government in medical ministry. They have asked him to be a

counselor to the medical staff because of his ministry to the lepers.

A Lady Who Became a Christian

On our way back to the convention centre we stopped at several of the preaching places where the evangelists are working. At one place we were invited to visit the home of a lady, who was a lady of some means. She had become a Christian by the witness of "The Little Bible of Salvation." She was involved in helping the mission get started in the village where we had our convention. The land where the tent had been set up had been purchased by the Mandapalli family as the future church home for the mission in this village. Already the families had gotten together and built a shelter of mud brick and bamboo sticks, which would be used as a church. On this occasion it was being used as a place to prepare food and to serve the many people who had come to the convention. Everybody was served a good meal each day, and, of course, I was expected to provide the food.

Evening Sessions

Convention services had been scheduled for the evening so that the working people could attend. Again I was to speak to the group, and either Peri or his brother, John, was to interpret for me. A bible quiz had been presented during the day. In the evening service there was to be recognition of the person who had scored the highest number of points.

Grandma in Heaven

As for the sermon, I don't remember the sermon as much, but as I moved along in the sermon I decided that I would make mention of Mother Mandapalli, who had been at the first convention. She had been well known to most of the evangelists and Bible women, for these people are quite closely related. There were at least three hundred people in the tent that evening. I said, "I observe that Mother Mandapalli, that is Grandma Mandapalli, is not with us. I presume that she has passed away. And I presume that she has gone to heaven. And I envision that every morning she asks the angels, 'Is he here yet?', as she had done before I arrived in India for the first convention. But as you can see, I have not gone to heaven yet. But someday I hope to be there. And I expect to see Mother Mandapalli. And we will be glad to see each other. I do not know what we will say to each other, because I do not speak any Telegu, and Mother Mandapalli did not speak any English. But we will be glad to be with the Lord Jesus." Of course, the people were glad that I should thus remember their grandmother. And I don't think that there is anything wrong by being a bit personal in our preaching. Everything I said was being interpreted, and it was also being recorded on two tape recorders, and the message was going out over the loud speakers. I am sure the people will long remember this service. But something happened the next day that I had not expected. The Hindu people who had gathered in the night stood outside of the tent looking in. There were probably three or four hundred of them. They were talking with the evangelists and Bible women the next day about what I had said in the sermon. For the first time in their lives they had heard someone speaking about knowing each other in the life to come, and of being in the presence of God. Both concepts are entirely foreign to the Hindu concept of life hereafter. Little did I realize as I was preaching to the faithful evangelists and Bible women that my message was being heard by the Hindu people outside of the tent. I might have known that they were listening because I could see their eyes shining in the darkness as they stood outside of the tent, but I was preaching only to the Christians in the tent. One never knows who is going to hear us when we preach, but the Lord "works His wonders to perform." Who knows what will come of such witness. But this I know, the evangelists had their work cut out for them the next day.

The Convention Comes to a Close
The following day we were to wind up our convention. There was the customary recognition of the outstanding workers, and of those who had helped to make the convention a success. Farewell speeches and plaques were presented to us for our part in the convention. And so the second convention of "The Little Bible of Salvation" came to a close.

Baptizing the Orphans
My work was not yet done. It had been planned that I should visit the orphanages and baptize the children. We were supporting three orphanages in this area at that time. The original orphanage was started by Peri, and the second one was started by his brother John, and a third one had been started in the village of Peddi Palem, where the bicycle evangelist had visited and distributed "The Little Bible of Salvation." The flood had come and the orphanage at Peddi Palem had been washed away. None of the children were lost. They were now staying in the other two orphanages which were already overcrowded. So the next morning they brought the children to the hotel where we were staying, that I should baptize them in our hotel room. Three or four of them would be in our room at a time. I would baptize them, and then others would come into the room. Some of the girls who had met me four years earlier wanted me to know that they knew me. They wanted to show me that they had learned some English. One of the girls stood next to me and said, "I'm a girl." I looked at her and said, "You can say that again." So she said, "I'm a girl." As I baptized them I spoke in English and Peri told them what I said in Telegu.

And Then There Were More

We had not finished with the baptism of these orphans when one of the evangelists came with 26 children which he had taken into his home. I had preached at his church the night before, but the service was so late that he did not ask me to baptize the children at his church. But now he had come with two taxis loaded with the children, and I baptized all 26 of them. Since then his orphanage has also become our concern, and we have support for 13 of these children.

In the afternoon we drove out into the country—I think it may have been 40 miles. But who can tell how many miles one travels in a taxi, when obviously we travel just as far up and down as we travel going forward. Here we came to brother John's orphanage. Again I was to preach for the children. This service was recorded and has been used many times by the evangelists. I remember that I spoke about Jesus, "The Good Shepherd," and how He loves the little children. After the services I was to baptize the children one after another. I do not remember how many children I baptized at each place, but I know that I baptized 84 children that day, and I was bushed.

Oh yes, these children, as well as the children at Kesavaram orphanage, were all presented with new clothes, dresses for the girls, and suits for the boys. Material had been provided by the people in the community, because the children had lost most of their clothes in the flood. The Mandapalli women had sewn the clothes, and Arda was to present each of the children with the gift of clothes. This was a day to remember.

Do People Eat Fish?

On the way back to the hotel we crossed over the canal where some men were fishing. I had asked Peri if the fish were good to eat. He assured me that they were. A man stood by the bridge with his catch of fish. So Peri ordered the cab driver to stop so he could buy the fish. Peri asked if the fish were for sale.

"Oh, yes."

"How much?"

"Twenty rupees."

"Too much. I give two rupees."

"No, twenty."

No sale. Peri got back into the cab, and shut the door. Soon the man rapped on the window of the cab. "Two rupees." And the deal was made. We went back to the hotel to rest. Peri took the fish to his mother's house. We had not seen his mother on this trip. She had not been feeling well, so she had not attended the convention. We were to go there for our evening meal. We waited and waited. It was past eleven o'clock and we were going out for dinner. I would much rather have gone to bed, but we would have to pay mother Mary a visit. On our way as we were driving along, a snake slithered across the road in front of us. The taxi came to a complete halt. There is no way that the cab driver would run over the snake, since he was a Hindu. I could understand that, but what I did not know is that it is against the law to kill a snake in India, or so we were told. We went on until we arrived at the Mandapalli home. We had to see the church that had been built since the first time that I was in India. It was a very modest building, but at least I could see that these people were intent upon doing something for themselves. This is good.

A Midnight Snack

We were to have our evening meal and it was already midnight. It was Peri's birthday. All of the family had come together for the celebration. Mother Mary had prepared the fish, and it was set before us. The family would not eat until we had eaten. I didn't feel like eating anything. Even the sound of the word "food" made me feel queasy. The fish looked good, but I wasn't hungry, and besides it was cooked with curry sauce. I think they use the curry sauce to cook the meat after the fire goes out. I tried to get Ammaji to eat some of the fish, but she would not eat. She took some of the fish in her fingers and held it to my mouth and said, "Eat." I said, "You eat." She said, "No, you eat," and she put the fish in my mouth. I had to eat. She kept taking the fish off the bones and putting it to my mouth, and I kept eating. Finally, the fish began to taste god even though it had curry sauce on it. My appetite began to come back to me, and between Arda and myself we did away with two pretty good sized fish. But the family did not eat while we were there.

A Gift to Remember

Peri wanted to present us with a special gift. A friend had carved a picture of the head of Christ out of wood. And this he presented to us. The craftsman who had done the carving was there also. He wanted to be in on the presentation of the gift. He wanted us to know that while he was working on the head of Christ, he had thought to himself that he should become a Christian, but "Not yet," he said, meaning that he had not yet become a Christian. But this shows the power of Jesus in as much as the person who was doing the carving would consider becoming a Christian.

Why Go to Bed?

We left the Mandipalli home long after midnight and went back to the hotel for a short nap. We were to get up early before daylight and drive to the train station at Rajahmundry to catch the early train for Visak. All of the Mandapalli family and many of their friends came in taxis to the station to say goodbye to us again.

One Can Dream

Peri went with us to Visak on the train. We stayed at Visak in a hotel for 24 hours of rest and recuperation. I should have made better use of my time, but I was constantly fighting the Delhi-belly. While we sat in the hotel Peri shared with us some of his ambitious dreams, namely, that our mission might continue to grow so that we might have a small church in every village in Andhra Pradesh and that we might have many orphanages and care homes, and a primary school in every village, and some secondary schools throughout the land. Like I said, this is an ambitious dream, but it shows that he had done some good thinking. It is surprising how many of the evangelists who have written to me since we returned home are thinking along the same line. And truly nothing is really going to happen to the People in India, until they accept the Christian religion, and begin to think more positively about themselves and their fellowmen.

CHAPTER SEVEN

Rest and Relaxation

On to Trivandrum

We had made plans to spend three days with our friends from the States in Trivandrum in Kerala State which is far south of our mission in Kesavaram. We flew from Visak to Hyderabad, from Hyderabad to Madras, and from Madras to Trivandrum. We spent ten times as much time waiting for the planes as we spent in the air. Each time we boarded a plane we had to pass through inspections. It seemed a never ending hassle. How good it was to see our friends who had come to the airport to meet us. We spent some leisure time at a hotel near the Indian Ocean. We went swimming every day in the ocean. It was great fun and very relaxing. We also spent some time at Trivandrum, where a lady by the name of Sumi has an orphanage, which the Neffs from Kansas help support.

This home was a paradise compared with what our people have in Andhra Pradesh. The standard of living is much higher in Kerala State. And, of course, it costs more to maintain the orphanage here. The children in this orphanage at least have a cot to sleep on.

A House That Could Be a Home

We visited the compound where Mrs. Neff had been born and raised. In my judgment I would say that the church had provided very well for our missionaries in the early days, for the house was certainly a mansion compared to other houses in India. In fact, we have never had the privilege of living in such a nice home in all of our years of ministry in the States. I mention this to cast no aspersions, but simply to say that our church has always made an effort to provide well for our missionaries, as well we should. But now the home is standing idle. When our missionaries returned from India it was not possible for the church to send replacements. No church has been able to send missionaries to India, since India got her freedom from Great Britain. They did however, permit the churches that were in existence to continue with their programs. Fortunately we had developed a ministry in South India and had a seminary for the training of native workers. Such work was not terminated. In some cases it has been possible to send in replacements as teachers, but the church cannot send in new missionaries to India. So the property where Mrs. Neff was born and raised has been standing idle except for such a time when it was rented. During that time it depreciated in value because there were no plans for the upkeep of the property. What a wonderful thing it would be if the church in India would use this property to maintain an orphanage, or even lease it to Sumi, so she could have adequate space for a larger orphanage. Here they could house up to one hundred orphans. I believe there are 19 acres of land in the compound. They would be able to cultivate the land and produce much of their own food. But our church as such has never launched out on a program of support for the orphans. Orphans are found all over India. We are still hoping that the India Evangelical Lutheran Church will do something with the property and let it become productive in regard to ministry for the people in India.

Language Barriers in India

I should say a bit about the difference that exists among the different states in India. In Kerala State about 28 percent of the people are Christians. In Andhra Pradesh less than six percent of the people are Christian. In some states less than one tenth of one percent of the people are Christian. In Kerala State the standard of living is much higher than in Andhra Pradesh. They speak a different language. For the church of South India to do mission work in other parts of India, it will be necessary for them to train people from these other places to work among their own people. Otherwise, it would be like the people of France trying to do mission work in Germany using the French language. The language barrier in India is a tremendous barrier. English is the official language of the country, only for convenience. The people prefer to speak in their own language. As more and more of the younger generation are receiving an education, and most of them will be able to converse in English, some of the language barriers will come tumbling down. But in the meantime it will be necessary to share the Gospel of salvation with the people in their own languages, so that the people might emerge with a united Christian witness. Otherwise the people will surely become communist. Already the communists are active in India. As the people become better educated the communists will say to the people, "If you want to improve your standard of living, join the party."

Why Do They Come?

We saw many Russians in India. We had seen many of them when we were in India on our first trip. A Russian was standing on the flight deck as we were leaving Visak. He was waving farewell to his comrades back at the hanger. I stepped out on the platform of the plane to wave goodbye to Peri and his friends. I spoke to this gentleman and asked him, "Do you speak English?" He replied in perfect English, "No, I do not speak English." So I asked him in German, "Sprecken sie aber Deutsch?" And he answered in perfect German, "Nein, Ich sprecke nicht Deutsch." Well, that ended our conversation. It was obvious that he had no intention of speaking with me. At Trivandrum at the hotel where we were staying out by the ocean for rest and relaxation a tour group arrived. As we sat eating our dinner they came in and sat at another table. Someone in our group wondered where they were from. I said, "No doubt they are from Russia." So I went over to their table and asked them. This time I received an answer. They were with a tour group from Russia to study the cultural development of the people of India. The man who answered me indicated that he was not interested in any further conversation. During the afternoon some of our ladies tried to strike up a conversation with their ladies, but they would not talk. It is as though they are afraid to be seen talking with anyone else. Later when we were on our way home we saw a lady at the airport in Bombay. She was traveling alone and was struggling with her baggage. I went over to her and spoke to her, seeing she could use some help. I asked her in German, "Sin sie Deutsch?" "Auch yah," she said. We had a friend from that moment until we parted company at Frankfurt. What a difference in people. She was a teacher from Calcutta and was going home to visit her mother in East Germany in Berlin. I had observed that there were many foreigners getting ready to board the plane at Bombay. It was quite obvious that these people were European. It was also quite obvious that they were not diplomats. Their clothing was very coarse and simple. I asked the lady that we had met if these people were Russian and she said they were. I asked her, "How can common laborers of Russia afford to make such a trip?" She

said, "They fill their luggage with vodka and sell it in India."
She said, "The custom officers do not even inspect their
luggage." Well, that was her story. I had noticed when we first
arrived in India that the officials did not inspect our luggage,
but every Indian that was on the flight had to pass through
inspection. Even the luggage of the pilot was thoroughly
inspected.

God Communicates With Everybody.

There must have been 240 people on this one flight going
back to Russia. Arda and I were the only Americans and the
lady from Germany was the only German. It did make us
wonder what so many of these people were doing in India,
that there should be so many of them on our flight. But who
are we to wonder, we would not have found out if we had
asked. They hardly spoke to one another. However, when we
flew over the Alps the next morning, they all got excited, for
the sun was shining, and the Alps are very beautiful. They
began to talk with each other and marvel at the beauty of the
Alps. They got their cameras out and took many pictures.
They even invited me to come to one of the windows so I
could take some pictures, also. I thought to myself, how
wonderful it is that God can soften people by the beauty of
nature, and strike a common bond between people who
seemingly have nothing in common. God is not so far
removed from people that He cannot reach out and touch
them.

Proper Farewell

Let me go back to Trivandrum for a moment. I would seem
that we just took off without saying goodbye to our friends.
We did part company at Trivandrum. The Neffs were going to
visit some other places in India, and they were going to come
back by way of Greece, and spend more time in Rome. We

stopped in Rome only to take on fuel for our flight to
Frankfurt. We were going to visit Denmark on our way home,
for this was the home of my parents, and I had never been in
Denmark. So we said our proper goodbyes at Trivandur, and
wished Sumi God's continued blessing on her work with the
orphans.

Traveling Can Be So Frustrating

When we left India I said, "How good it is that we will not
have to hassle with the coolies again." When we got to
Frankfurt we were absolutely on our own, and we were
saying, "If only we could find some coolie to carry our
luggage for us." Now it was do it yourself if you expect to get
there. I was able to speak German well enough so that we
were able to make the exchange from the airport to the train
terminal, and to get on the right train. What little German I
had learned at the seminary 40 years earlier stood me in good
stead.

When our train came to Denmark, they changed the crew,
and immediately I had to change my language and speak
Danish. What fun this was because the German language
insisted on coming out ahead of the Danish.

We arrived in Aalborg late at night. The caretaker of the
depot was closing the doors. I had gone to find a cab. Arda
was left outside in the cold with the luggage. She was not
favorably impressed with such a reception, for she was put
out of the depot and was told she could not stay there.
Fortunately she was not able to express her disgust since she
does not speak any Danish.

The People Care

It is a very beautiful country. It is kept very clean. Every bit
of land is put to productive use. Many buildings were heated
by hot water. In Aalborg, a city of 100,000 people, they have

one central heating plant. Hot water is piped to all the buildings in the city. Some of the people also use auxiliary solar heat. There is virtually no pollution in Aalborg. Let me also mention that the people of Denmark are concerned about their national security yet they have only a small army and navy. They could not protect themselves against any aggressor. They are very happy when our nation is strong and carries respect among the nations of this world. When President Kennedy was our president the people of Denmark were very happy. They even named streets in the towns after John F. Kennedy.

Then there came a time in the history of our country that we had lost considerable prestige and respect among the nations of the world. During that time the people of Denmark lived in fear because they know that they cannot protect themselves. But once again they feel comfortable knowing that we have regained considerable prestige among the nations of the world.

Influenza They Call It

I did not make the best use of my time in Denmark, as I was still fighting the Delhi-belly, and by this time I had also contracted influenza. I spent most of my time recuperating under goose-down blankets. Arda was most uncomfortable because she could not join in the conversation with the people. When Soren Niss came home from a stay in Canada and a visit to the States, he was able to translate for us, and Arda had someone to interpret for her. I could have done more of this, but I was usually so busy trying to figure out what they were saying and trying to visit with them that I forgot to interpret for her.

We left Denmark and went to London only to spend the next 24 hours at the hotel Aerial. I spent the whole 24 hours in bed recuperating so that we would be able to make the trip home the next day. What a way to see London. They did however, have a closed circuit TV showing us what was going on in London all of the time.

How good it was to get back home. Our son Ted met us at O'Hare airport in Chicago and drove us back to Springfield. Pastor Kaufmann was good to me in that he gave me time to recuperate before he asked me to resume my responsibilities in the parish at Springfield.

CHAPTER EIGHT

What Now?

Evaluation

But now came the time for re-evaluation. I had made the second trip because I wanted to see how the mission was developing. I was aware that there was no direct responsibility on the part of anyone to anyone, other than the director was responsible to me, and we live 12,000 miles away. I had observed that there were as many as 125 evangelists and 40 Bible women working in our mission which was an increase of 500 percent in the past four years. I observed that there was very little supervision. There was no direct line of responsibility. I observed that it would be possible for the evangelists to go off in 125 different directions in their teaching. I promised before I left India that I would prepare a book of "Basic Christian Doctrine," for the people and I would do that immediately. I set to work on this immediately and I recall that I had completed the book on the 4th of July, 1984. This was a cause for celebration, or at least a day to remember. The manuscript was sent to India for translation into Telegu. I estimated that we could use as many as 4,000 copies of the book almost immediately, certainly within the next four years. And if things develop as they have been, that we could use another 10,000 in 10 years.

An Unexpected Visitor

In June 1984 we had an unexpected visitor from India. He had been on a mission in Malaysia, Indonesia and Singapore during the time that we were in India, so he did not see us at that time. He has found many Telegu speaking people in this part of Southeast Asia. He is wanting to start a mission among them. I told him that I was working on a manuscript to provide a book of basic Christian doctrine for our evangelists in India, and that it was our intention to have it translated into the Telegu language for the people. I asked him if he would approve the translation for us and help us get it published. He examined the manuscript, as far as it had been written at that time, and said he would be glad to review the translation. He also said that he would see to it that it got published. When I told him we might need as many as 4,000 copies, he said, "You don't need 4,000, you need 100,000." He called me sometime later from Kansas City and said, "You don't have to worry about the book, it will be published." At that time he asked permission to publish "The Little Bible of Salvation" in limited quantity for use in his ministry in various languages in India. Of course, I gave him permission. He asked me if I would come over to India to help him set up a pre-seminary training for the evangelists. I told him he did not realize what he was asking of me. I do not have such expertise, nor do I have any experience along that line. I would say however, that this is perhaps the greatest need for the Christian ministry in India. We must go with the native Indians in Christian ministry, and we must go with them now. We cannot afford to wait until they all have a chance to earn a Ph.D. They are already involved in Christian witness, but they desperately need some guidance. Anyhow, the evangelists are most anxious for the "Book of Basic Christian Doctrine" to be published so that they can use it to teach the people. There is no question that we can use 4,000 copies of the book right now, and within ten years we can use another 10,000 in our mission in and around the Kesavaram area. I just now talked with Pastor Vijaya Rao. He said the book will be published by July 1st. He wants to take 2,000 copies with him when he visits the South China islands this summer.

To Train a Ministry

Although it had been approved by officials of our synod that Peri should come to this country and prepare for ministry, this has not materialized. It was required of him that he prepare some lessons by correspondence, because he has had no formal training in religion. He has completed two of these courses and did a remarkably good job with his studies. He has not completed the third course because the work load has increased month by month in India. He has been trying to keep in touch with all the 125 evangelists and the 40 Bible women, and provide overall supervision of the four orphanages. Through generous gifts of our people we were able to provide a motor scooter for him, so that he could get around to visit the evangelists and help conduct meetings. The need has not changed. It is even more important today that he be given a chance to upgrade his theological study, so that in turn he might be able to upgrade the teaching of the evangelists. The one thing that is imperative for the future of the mission is that the evangelists develop the best possible spirit of cooperation. They must develop some sense of responsibility not toward a hierarchical system, but to a strong program of development based upon mutual acceptance and support of each other. Presently I am recommending that Peri receive his theological training at our seminary in Nagercoil, India. This would cost far less and might establish a good relationship with our India Evangelical Lutheran Church of South India. When and if Peri should go to school at a seminary we have arranged that his brother John would supervise the work in the Kesavaram area.

More and More Ask to Join

The mission is not limited to the 125 evangelists and 40 Bible women that attended our conference in 1983. Since we have returned to the States we have received many letters from people who want to become a part of our ministry. They ask to receive "The Little Bible of Salvation" so they can take it out to the villages and teach the people from it. Many of them tell of Hindu people becoming Christian by virtue of this witness. We know that it is the Spirit of God that bears witness through the Word of God that brings about a conversion. Yet is is brought about by the people listening to people. Almost every day we receive a letter from someone who wants to work with the mission. Some days we receive as many as seven letters.

Some See Visions

One day I received two letters on the same day. The letters were very similar. It was as though they had taken a letter to the church secretary and asked her to run off a duplicate copy. Both letters began by each evangelist saying he had had a vision during the night. Each had seen me flying through space with the angels. And all Andhra Pradesh was becoming Christian. Then they would plead with me that I should come over to India and make this possible. At the end of each letter they included affidavits which people had signed stating that they had become Christians by virtue of the witness of "The Little Bible of Salvation." Now I have always been a bit skeptical of people who claim to have seen visions. But this shook me a bit that I should receive two such letters on the same day from two people in India. These people had no way of knowing each other, because they were from different parts of the country. I am not about to tell them that they did not see a vision, for if the Lord should send them a vision, who am I to say the Lord did not do this. I have a strong feeling that these people are so anxious to bring the Gospel to their people and that their desire is so intense that they envision something like this until it actually becomes a vision. These people would not know me if they should see me flying through space, because they have never seen me. I told Arda that it is not necessary for me to go to India in order that all Andhra should become Christian. If I went over there I would be in only one place at a time. But through "The Little Bible of Salvation" and the many evangelists and Bible women who are asking to work with the Little Bible, the message is getting to the people of Andhra. We have distributed 240,000 booklets in the Telegu language in the past seven years. In India it is estimated that at least ten people receive the message from each booklet that is sent. So it is possible that 2 million and 400,000 people have heard of God's salvation by way of the little booklet. But what is that in a country where there are 90 million people who speak the Telegu language and more than 700,000,000 who speak other languages and dialects.

Reaching Out in Other Languages

The booklet has also been translated in seven other languages in India. Two weeks ago I received a request for copies in Koya. Just yesterday I received a request for the booklet in Lambadi. Both of these languages are dialect languages spoken in Andhra Pradesh. What we need to do is publish and distribute 10 million copies of the booklet in Telegu and that would just be a beginning. There are some 24 major languages in India and 1600 dialects. There are more than 700 million people in India. It is possible to reach these people in their own language by using "The Little Bible of Salvation." We must strike while the iron is hot. Right now it is hot in Andhra Pradesh. I thank God every day for the Lutheran Braille workers who have made the booklet available in large print in eight different languages for the people in India. They have also promised to publish it in as many languages in which it might be translated.

Another Mission in India

And now let me tell you about one of the Bible women who made contact with us since we were in India. Her name is Mrs. Argan Rose. Not only did she write and ask for help, they all ask for help, but somehow she conveyed a sense of urgency and personal concern so that I decided to send her a bit of help. Soon we had received pictures of her thirty orphans. Gradually we solicited help for some of her children. Each month we send money for nine of the children. I wish we had support for all of them. Of course, the money is used to buy food so that all of the children may eat. A few months later she expressed a desire to start a Christian school for the orphans and the neighborhood children. She asked for my advice. I could not say, "No," but I could not give her any encouragement. I guess since I did not say "no" she took it that she should proceed. She contacted the government authorities and they encouraged her to start such a school. She found four Christian women who were willing to teach for $20.00 a month. She found a man who would qualify and serve as headmaster. He would serve for $30.00 a month. She had a bit of money, an inheritance which amounted to $1,000. This she used to buy some land, and to begin building a four room school. By the first of November she was ready to begin school. By January 1 of this year the enrollment of the school had reached 156 and more people were asking to send their children. They met on people's verandas, or out under some trees, or in the shade of some buildings, but they are having school. We still need about $2,500 to complete the school

86

building. Her interest in Christian education comes from the fact that her father was a Lutheran teacher in India.

This could become one of the most significant developments of our mission in India. Education is highly regarded by the people of India. And it seems that the government is willing to encourage such a ministry. It might even be that the government would allow us to send in teachers from this country, even though at this time we cannot send in missionaries. What we would need to do is find teachers that would be willing to teach for $20.00 a month, and teach as many as 40 children. It is a different world over there, and of course, we could not expect our teachers to teach for $20.00 a month, so we must go with the Christian teachers that we find in India. Neither can we build a four room schoolhouse for $3,900 to take care of 156 children.

At this time I want to introduce you to Mrs. Argan Rose, and her staff of teachers. Headmaster, S. Chitti Rabu; teacher, Baby Siromani; teacher,.B. Bay Sarojini; teacher, Jyothi Subhadra; and teacher Ch. Aruma Kumari. They are teaching in English and in Telegu. You should also see the children of the school.

Yet Another Mission

Who knows what is next? About three months ago I received a letter from a Bible woman, who wanted me to suggest a name for her little daughter. She was also asking to become a part of our working team, and was asking for "The Little Bible of Salvation." I sent her some booklets and thought I would suggest that she name her daughter "Arda." A month later we received a letter from her in which she thanked us for the use of Arda's name for her little girl. But now she had also given Arda's name to the orphanage. It is called Arda's Children's Home. It is thus officially registered with the government of India. There she is taking care of 25 children. I kid my wife and ask her how it feels to become a mother of 25 children all at once at her age. Well, she is taking it all in stride, and eventually she will find 25 people who will help support these children at $10.00 a month.

Most recently this lady asked us to help her establish a sewing centre so she could train the young girls so that they could learn the trade and be able to provide an income for

88

themselves. She has called the sewing centre "Arda's Sewing Centre," which is a joke because Arda doesn't sew. But the sewing centre is already in existence. This young woman is a very capable person and handles her English very well. If we wanted to sponsor another Christian school all we would have to do is suggest it, and she would see to it that it became a reality.

We Can All Do Something

Most of the people who write to us are struggling with their English as it is not quite the same as ours. We now have support for children living in ten different homes, and half a dozen others have asked us to establish support for their orphans. Sometimes we become frustrated, because there seems to be no end. We certainly cannot take care of all the orphans in India, but we can take care of one at a time. And if others will sponsor a child it will make a difference. Our first concern is that the money which people give is all sent and used for whatever purpose it is given. Our second concern is that the children have an opportunity to grow up as Christians. This, of course, will make a great difference in the life of each child. It can also make a great difference in regard to the future of Christianity in India. But most important is that the basic Christian faith and the knowledge of God's salvation is shared with the people.

This is not the end of the story. It is just the beginning. I hope that the story will not come to an end, but that it may continue to be written as the Lord God provides a Christian witness for these people, and as these people share the witness with each other.

CHAPTER NINE

Addenda

One at a Time

I would like to share with you an addenda, to show you how the people are responding to this particular mission. Everywhere we have had an opportunity to share the story someone or some group has come forth with support for the mission. Most of the support is in the form of continuing monthly support of the orphans. Monthly support hurts the least, and does the most good. Most people do not have $120 lying around waiting to be spent, and would not want to give that much at any one time to support an orphan, yet they have little difficulty in giving $10.00 a month for a child.

Children Love to Help Children

Some people begin by supporting one orphan and find so much joy in this that they ask to support another child. Let me tell you about the children in one of our Lutheran schools in Illinois. They began to support a child. They brought weekly offerings and they sent their monthly support of $10. At the end of the school year, they sent their monthly support of $10. At the end of the school year, they sent an additional check in the amount of $556. Their additional support would take care of another four children. This became a real blessing for the children in India, but I could not help but think of how much good this project had done for the children of Immanuel School at Rock Island, Illinois. God bless them.

Something to Live For

One dear lady in a care home had seen the pictures and asked to talk with me about support for the children. When I presented her with a picture of a little boy she was so happy that she cried. Each month she sends her check in the amount of $10.00 to support her child. I stopped by to visit her when I came through her town. She was so glad to see me. I said, "I'll bet you never thought you would have a little boy at your age." She was so proud of her little boy. She really had nothing to look forward to in the nursing home, but to stare at the four walls of her room, but now she has her little boy. The most important day of each month is when the nurses bring her check book and she can write her check for her little boy May God keep her happy.

A Special Project — We Call Her Missy

Sometime ago I mentioned a possible mission project to our nephew, Curt Bach, and his wife, Teresa. They are living on a ranch at Chadron, Nebraska. They had expressed some interest in supporting the mission. I suggested that we might buy a heifer and they might feed her and let her raise a calf and they could then sell the calf and give the money for the mission. This they agreed to do. But before we could purchase the heifer a friend of ours had a calf that had lost its mother and he offered to give it to Curt. Curt accepted the gift and called the calf Missy, because she belongs to the mission.

He would keep her and let her raise a calf each year for the mission. Since no money was being made available for the mission until the calf grew up and raised a calf, they decided they would begin to support the

mission by sending $10.00 a month for one of the orphans. They told some of their friends and they likewise are supporting an orphan. So the Lord provides and He adds His blessings every day. The best is yet to come!

Gifts to The Little Bible of Salvation Foundation may be sent directly to either of the following:

The First Bank of Apache   or   Reverend J. Einar Bach
Apache, Oklahoma 73006   2604 Timothy Terrace
                                   Bethany, MO 64424

To support orphans or evangelists contact any of the following:

Reverend J. Einar Bach
2604 Timothy Terrace
Bethany, MO 64424

Jan and Ray Huebner
RR 3 Box 98
Falls City, NB 68355

Ted and Alice Bach
1437 Tomahawk Lane
Olathe, KS 66061

Clifford and Phyllis Bach
Box 365
Trenton, NB 69044

Rev. Philip Bach
909 - 8th Ave N
Glasgow, MT 59230

Harold and Irene Huebner
2602 Chase
Falls City, NB 68355

Alice and Leon Seebeck
Verdon, OK 73092

Joe and Frieda Hanson
603 NE 5th
Madison, SD 57042

Doane and Betty Mortenson
Howard, SD 57349

Lawrence & Mildred Petrosky
310 2NE
Wessington Spgs, SD 57382

Wilmar Schwarzrock
RR 1
Gaylord, MN 55334

Donald and Cleone Neff
RR 1 Box 4
Lakin, KS 67860

Rev. & Mrs. Albert Schudde
1119 Poplar
Buhl, ID 83316

Violetta Markert
401 1/2 W. Elliott
Springfield, IL 62702